THE COMPLE
AIR FRYER COOKBOOK

Written by: Rebecca Jones

Copyright © 2018

All Rights Reserved

All rights reserved. No part of this book may be reproduced or transmitted in any form or by any means, electronic or mechanical, including photocopying, recording or by any information storage and retrieval system, without written permission from the publisher, except for the inclusion of brief quotations in a review.

Warning-Disclaimer

The purpose of this book is to educate and entertain. The author or publisher does not guarantee that anyone following the techniques, suggestions, tips, ideas, or strategies will become successful. The author and publisher shall have neither liability or responsibility to anyone with respect to any loss or damage caused, or alleged to be caused, directly or indirectly by the information contained in this book.

Contents

INTRODUCTION

Are you trying to live a healthy and happy life? Do you want to improve your eating habits but still struggle with self-control and diets? If you answered "Yes", do not panic! You are not alone; many of us struggle with a long-term weight loss and healthy eating. With so many diets, kitchen appliances, cookbooks, and different information, it is difficult to know what to focus on.

An Air Fryer has come to solve this issue! With its exceptional and advanced technology, it will shape the future of cooking and dieting. To be healthy and happy right now does not require a lot of time, money or sacrifice. It requires just a little motivation and the right information. This unique and innovative kitchen appliance uses the power of superheated air to cook food in a specially engineered cooking basket, by providing you and your family with healthier options every day. Luckily, a modern technology improves daily lives, making it easier and better!

There is no magic wand, but remember that the right dietary regimen and persistence can do wonders! A ketogenic diet promotes healthy food choices for a lifetime; instead of following rigid dietary rules and unrealistic weight-loss goals, simply embrace good eating habits. After all, you are what you eat.

The Ketogenic Diet in a Nutshell

A ketogenic diet is low in carbohydrates and high in fats, which results in weight loss and improved health. The primary goal of a ketogenic diet is to get your body into the state of ketosis, which is a natural, metabolic state.

According to Wikipedia, ketosis is a "metabolic state in which some of the body's energy supply comes from ketone bodies in the blood, in contrast to a state of glycolysis in which blood glucose provides energy."

It means your body uses ketones for energy instead of glucose, and consequently, it becomes a fat-burner instead of a sugar-burner.

You can achieve this goal by simply avoiding carbs and eating protein food and healthy fats instead. How does that sound to you? Can you do this? No matter how easy and healthy it may be, you should follow some general rules in order to achieve the best results and stay healthy during a ketogenic diet. Since many common ingredients contain carbohydrates, it can be tricky. However, it is possible to eat low-carb food every day in the long term. When you buy groceries, read labels carefully to make sure that a certain product can fit into your low-carb diet.

Since your body needs over 45 different nutrients on a daily basis, you should follow the recommended macronutrient ratio. It means, to balance your diet, you should eat 5–10 percent of calories from carbs, 15–30 percent of calories from protein, and 60–75 percent of calories from fat.

What to eat on a ketogenic diet:

VEGETABLES – non-starchy veggies and pickled vegetables (preferably homemade).

MEAT & POULTRY – any type. The fat on the meat is also allowed.

FISH & SEAFOOD – any type. Fatty fish such as salmon, sardines or herring are a good choice.

DAIRY PRODUCTS – opt for full-fat cheese, yogurt, and milk. A cream (40% fat) and butter are great on a ketogenic diet. Be careful with skim milk as it usually contains a lot of sugar.

EGGS – poached, scrambled, deviled, boiled, fried, omelets, hard-boiled, all kinds are allowed.

NATURAL FAT – organic oil, butter, cream; feel free to experiment and try high-fat sauces such as Hollandaise sauce. Coconut oil and olive oil are the best options for everyone not only for keto dieters.

NUTS – the best options are Brazil, macadamia and pecan nuts. You can use a nut butter too, but be careful with a store-bought butter; make your own homemade peanut or almond butter.

FRUITS – you can eat berries in moderation.

DRINKS – water, regular or sparkling; black coffee with a full-fat cream (without sugar, of course); tea. For instance, if you added a sugar cube to your coffee, you can take 4 grams of carbs and that is not good for your diet. Wine is good in moderation since a serving size (about 5 ounces) contains 2 grams of carbohydrates. One cup of coconut water contains 9 grams of carbohydrates; you can always enjoy something else with no carbs at all but this is just for illustration purposes.

SWEETENERS – erythritol, monk fruit, stevia, and other sweeteners with a low glycemic index.

You cannot eat: grains rice, sugar, beans, legumes, and starchy vegetables.

•

Top Benefits of a Ketogenic Diet

1. **A healthy lifestyle…here we come!**

   Going into a state of ketosis not only reduces your insulin levels but it helps you control your blood sugar. When you eat lots of carbs, primarily found in pasta, bread, and sugary foods, it causes your body to produce a lot of insulin and glucose. Insulin is the chemical that helps your body turn glucose into energy. On the other hand, if you avoid carbs, your body will break down fats instead of carbs, which leads to more energy for daily activities.

   It can help you lower triglycerides that are stored in your fat cells. Nutritionists and physicians recommend eating fatty fish and healthy fats (peanut butter, avocado, seeds, and nuts) to reduce the risk of stroke. A keto diet can help reduce the symptoms of heart disease, Parkinson's disease

   Alzheimer's disease, migraines, and inflammation. Impressive!

   Here is one more advantage of a healthy diet – the more real foods you include in your diet, such as organic vegetables and pasture-raised meat, the better. The quality of your food matters so a ketogenic diet promotes whole, unprocessed food.

2. **This lifestyle boosts brain function.**

   The state of ketosis improves brain function, eliminating brain fog and lack of focus. This metabolic state balances the neurotransmitters in the brain. In addition, it improves mental focus, clarity and productivity. Due to the reduction of glucose, you will be able to reduce stress and anxiety. Added benefits of ketosis are better cognitive function and improved concentration.

3. **A natural way to lose weight.**

   As you probably already know, your body needs a constant supply of energy from the food. As mentioned above, carbs produce insulin and glucose, which causes fat to be stored in your cells instead of being burnt. When you avoid carbs, your body produces far lesser amounts of glucose and the state of ketosis kick starts! When your cells don't have access to glucose, they use fat for energy. It means that your fat cells just shrink and you can kick-start weight loss. This is also a great way to reduce excessive appetite automatically so you will need fewer calories. You will also get rid of cravings for junk food and sugary snacks.

4. **An easy way to improve energy levels and sleep better.**
Almost without exception, if you avoid carbs, your body will break down fat instead of carbs, which leads to more energy for daily activities. Moreover, researchers have found that a ketogenic dieting improves the quality of sleep naturally by enhancing slow-wave sleep.

Here are a few extra tips that might come in handy especially when you're just starting out.
- Focus on a clear protein, whole food and natural products and you'll be just fine.
- Take it easy, give yourself about two to three weeks to adjust to a diet; your body will thank you.
- Replenish electrolytes with a homemade bone broth. You can do this by simply adding salt to your drinking water as well.
- Meal planning and meal prep are vital to your long-term success on any diet, including a low-carb one.
- Stay determined – wherever you go, make sure you have ketogenic-approved food on hand. We cannot emphasize enough the importance of preparing to ensure success on a diet.
- Keep it simple by preparing meals in bulk and freeze them for the week; or you can eat the same thing for dinner a few times and pack leftovers for the next day's lunch.
- Flavor foods with seasonings instead of using sauces or gravy with flour.
- Stay hydrated. Always.
- Always consult your physician before beginning any dietary program.

Is there a foolproof system for cooking healthy, ketosis-inducing meals? Two words: AIR FRYER!

Before You Buy that Air Fryer:
How it Works?

If you just could not stand the idea of avoiding fried food, but you don't like all those extra calories that you take with it, air frying may become a long-term solution for you!

The Air Fryer makes your everyday cooking convenient and healthy by using revolutionary hot air cooking technology. Besides frying, air fryers allow you to roast vegetables, bake cakes, grill steaks, and steam delicate vegetables and seafood. The Air Fryer produces meals that are exceptionally healthy, quick, and flavorful; it pushes the limits of imagination. Incredible!

What is the secret behind excellent air fried fish, chips, and cakes? How can you make healthy fried food as good as professional chefs? It is called Rapid Air Technology. The Air Fryer heats up quickly; then, hot air swirls in the specialized chamber, cooking food evenly, using a minimum amount of fat. Your food cooks in its own natural juices so it retains its natural taste, texture and nutrients. The result is perfectly cooked food that tastes good and looks great on your table. All this without having to deep fry your food in a large quantity of oil. Any food that can be cooked in an oven, microwave or toaster, can be cooked in your Air Fryer.

Thanks to an automatic temperature control, you just have to set your device and you can be assured that your food will be cooked to perfection. How does it work in practice? Spritz a removable cooking basket with a nonstick cooking spray. Place your ingredients in the cooking basket and set your desired temperature; then, wait for the buzzer to signal the end of cooking.

There are some genius cooking tips from professional chefs that will help you to get the most out of your Air Fryer.

- To keep foods from sticking to the interior of the cooking basket, simply brush the bottom and sides with a cooking oil. It is also important for an easy cleanup.
- If you want a crispy surface on your vegetables, spritz them with a nonstick oil in the cooking basket.
- Never overfill the cooking basket.
- Clean your Air Fryer after every use; wipe the outside of the Air Fryer with a moist cloth and clean the cooking basket with hot water and dish detergent.
- You can use oven-safe dishes in your Air Fryer and bake the best cakes and frittatas ever. Make sure to check with the manual before using a new bakeware.
- Make sure to test your food for doneness because cooking times vary depending on the Air Fryer model. You can use a food thermometer.
- You can prepare frozen foods in your Air Fryer machine; just make sure to follow the cooking chart.
- You can use your Air Fryer to reheat ingredients by setting the temperature to 300 degrees F for up to 10 minutes.

How You'll Benefit from an Air Fryer

1. **No grease, fewer calories.**

   After detailed discussion, the International Food Research Journal concluded "The present results that the oil uptake was lower under air-frying confirming that this technique can be considered as a healthy one. Thus, this method must be practically process applied to obtain healthy fried foods."

   Realistically speaking, we love the taste of fried foods but not the mess and excess fat. Studies have shown that oils release toxic chemicals at high temperatures; these toxins can be a trigger for serious health problems such as cancer, high cholesterol, diabetes, and obesity. This is a health-conscious way to cook favorite foods using olive oil, coconut oil, and butter. In comparison to deep frying, air fryers produce food with about 80 percent less fat!

2. **Flavors, please!**

   Air frying is an exceptional way to fry foods using a hot air and it doesn't mean skimping on flavor. Thanks to the hot sealed environment, valuable nutrients are conserved and the flavors are richer and stronger. If you thought there is no such thing as a healthy fried food, this book will change your mind.

   You don't need a cluttered kitchen with so many fancy cookware. You don't need any special culinary skills. Air frying requires little effort, making it one of the hottest food trends for the coming year!

3. **An easy press-and-go operation will save you a tone of time.**

   With this revolutionary "fix-it and forget-it" system, air-fried meals practically cook themselves. Busy moms will be delighted! They require just a little prep and voilà – dinner is ready in minutes! From here on out, you can cook an entire meal using a super-heated air. There is the Air Fryer divider that allows you to cook two different types of food; just make sure to follow the cooking chart. It is fast, convenient, and easy to use. Fish fillets, chicken nuggets, French fries, cakes and other "greasy" foods are back on the menu! Moreover, you will end up with only one cooking basket for cleaning. The Air Fryer keeps your kitchen clean and pleasant; there is no smell and no mess!

4. **An effective weight loss trick.**

   If you are searching for a cooking method that can help you get a flat tummy, an Air Fryer may become your first choice. If you tend to boost flavors and cut calories, you just need to select the right cooking technique. Thanks to the Air Fryer, you will enjoy your favorite fried food and lose weight at the same time. You don't have to avoid saucy steaks, luscious cheesecakes, and French fries. You just need a kitchen device that can help you make the most of your food. This incredible machine allows you to enjoy nourishing, great-tasting and well-balanced meals without excess calories.

   Simply put, a controlled cooking time and a super-heated environment are key factors to a healthier cooking and more successful dieting. A hot air is a new oil; you should cut fat and calories not flavor! All these benefits make an Air Fryer the right option when it comes to healthy and enjoyable eating.

A Word about Our Recipe Collection

This recipe collection contains 135 simple yet tasty recipes that are divided into 10 categories. In addition to the surprising variety of great ketogenic recipe, this cookbook is chock-full of cooking secrets, serving ideas, tips and tricks for better air frying.

You will find timeless recipes, from quick and easy vegan meals to slurp-worthy stews and elegant dessert. All the recipes are written in an easy-to-follow way that will guide you every step of the way in order to prepare the best keto meals ever. The recipes are accompanied by nutritional information so you will be able to track your nutrition and count carbs. This recipe collection is designed to help you create homemade restaurant-quality meals easily and effortlessly even on those busy weeknights.

If you are tired of dieting, experimenting with too many weight-management strategies, the Air Fryer will transform your life. You will be surprised what this innovative device can do in the kitchen. Get started with the best ketogenic Air Fryer recipes that follow. Enjoy!

POULTRY

1. Za'atar Chicken Fillets with Chili Mayo

(Ready in about 35 minutes | Servings 4)

Chicken fillets are one of the favorite main dishes that cook perfectly in the Air Fryer. Chicken fillets and chili mayo combine very well so this family dish is attractive in appearance too.

Per serving: 422 Calories; 23.2g Fat; 6.6g Carbs; 43.8g Protein; 2.1g Sugars

Ingredients

For the Chicken Fillets:

3 teaspoons pork rinds

1 ½ teaspoons Za'atar seasonings

1 pound chicken fillets

1 yellow onion, sliced

2 garlic cloves, smashed

1 ¼ cups chicken broth, preferably
   homemade

2 sprigs rosemary, leaves picked

For the Homemade Chili Mayo:

1/2 cup mayonnaise

2 tablespoons sour cream

1 teaspoon stone ground mustard

1 tablespoon chipotle chili sauce

Directions

- In a shallow bowl, mix the pork rinds with Za'atar seasonings. Toss the chicken with this mixture mixture until it is well coated.
- Preheat your Air Fryer to 360 degrees F. Spritz the baking dish with a nonstick cooking spray or brush with 1 teaspoon of olive oil.
- Arrange the seasoned chicken fillets in a baking dish.
- Cook for 25 minutes, flipping the chicken fillets once. Lower the temperature on the Air Fryer to 340 degrees F.
- Add the remaining ingredients for the chicken fillets. Cook an additional 8 minutes.
- Meanwhile, make the homemade chili mayo by whisking mayonnaise, sour cream, mustard and chili sauce. Serve with warm chicken fillets.

2. Sunday Cheesy Turkey Fillets

(Ready in about 50 minutes | Servings 4)

Turkey fillets inspire us in so many ways! In this Air Fryer recipe, they're coated with Romano cheese and cornflakes and topped with Colby cheese.

Per serving: 681 Calories; 60.1g Fat; 5.9g Carbs; 26g Protein; 0.1g Sugars

Ingredients

Nonstick cooking spray

1/4 cup Romano cheese, freshly grated

1/4 cup cornflakes

1 ½ tablespoons olive oil

1 pound turkey fillets, sliced into 4 pieces

1/4 cup Colby cheese, shredded

Directions

- Preheat your Air Fryer to 350 degrees F for a couple of minutes. Spritz the cooking basket with a nonstick cooking spray.
- Combine Romano cheese and cornflakes in a shallow dish. Brush the turkey with olive oil.
- Now, dip each piece of turkey into cheese/cornflakes mixture. Cook in the preheated Air Fryer for 20 minutes.
- Flip the turkey fillets and cook on the other side for 15 minutes longer. The internal temperature should reach 165 degrees F.
- Lastly, top with shredded Colby cheese and cook 3 to 4 minutes more or until cheese is melted.
- Let the turkey fillets rest for 6 to 7 minutes before serving. Bon appétit!

3. Mexican-Style Turkey Delight

(Ready in about 30 minutes | Servings 6)

When it comes to the breadcrumb substitutes, you can use crushed pork rinds. It is a smart way to stay on a keto diet.

Per serving: 313 Calories; 18.7g Fat; 4.6g Carbs; 30.2g Protein; 2g Sugars

Ingredients

1 teaspoon olive oil

1 ½ pounds turkey breasts, cubed

1 egg, beaten

1/3 cup pork rinds

1 tablespoon olive oil

1 bell pepper, deveined and sliced

1 chili pepper, chopped

1 cup cauliflower florets

1/2 cup leek, sliced

2 garlic cloves, minced

1/4 cup dry white wine

1 tablespoon soy sauce

Directions

- Preheat your Air Fryer to 390 degrees F. Brush a cooking basket with 1 teaspoon of olive oil.
- Then, coat cubed turkey breasts with beaten egg, and lastly, dip into crushed pork rinds.
- Cook turkey breasts at 390 degrees F for 20 minutes.
- Meanwhile, preheat a sauté pan over a moderately high heat. Heat 1 tablespoon of olive oil until sizzling.
- Now, sauté the vegetables, gradually adding a dry white wine, until they are tender to your liking. Heat off. Add the soy sauce and stir to combine.
- Add air-fried turkey and stir until everything is well incorporated. Serve immediately with mustard and horseradish mayo.

4. Classic Shiritaki Noodles with Meat Sauce
(Ready in about 30 minutes | Servings 4)

Here is a classic family recipe that you can prepare for any occasion! Shiritaki Noodles contain only 1 gram of carbs per serving size.

Per serving: 200 Calories; 10.8g Fat; 5.9g Carbs; 19.9g Protein; 2.1g Sugars

Ingredients

1/2 leek, chopped
2 garlic cloves, minced
1/2 pound turkey, ground
1/2 pound chicken, ground
1/2 teaspoon flaky sea salt
1/4 teaspoon ground black pepper

1/2 teaspoon smoked cayenne pepper
1 teaspoon dried oregano
1/2 teaspoon dried rosemary
1/2 teaspoon dried basil
2 ripe tomatoes, crushed
1 (7-ounce) shiritaki noodles

Directions

- Start by preheating your Air Fryer to 380 degrees F.
- Add the leek, garlic, turkey, and chicken to your Air Fryer. Cook for 10 minutes.
- Add the salt, black pepper, cayenne pepper, oregano, rosemary, basil, and tomatoes. Cook an additional 15 minutes.
- In a large, deep pan, bring a lightly-salted water to a rolling boil. Boil noodles, stirring periodically to keep pasta from sticking to the bottom of your pan.
- Once cooked, drain noodles well. Serve with hot Bolognese sauce. Bon appétit!

5. Chinese-Style Parmesan Crusted Chicken

(Ready in about 35 minutes | Servings 6)

Here is the recipe for famous crunchy, parmesan-coated chicken drumsticks. Serve with vegetable fries and salad.

Per serving: 356 Calories; 21.8g Fat; 5.4g Carbs; 32.8g Protein; 0.8g Sugars

Ingredients

1 teaspoon sesame oil

2 tablespoons lime juice

1/4 cup Chinese cooking wine

2 tablespoons tamari sauce

2 tablespoons pureed tomato

1 tablespoon sambal oelek

2 cloves garlic, minced

6 chicken drumsticks

3/4 cup almond flour

1 teaspoon salt

1/2 teaspoon smoked cayenne pepper

1/2 teaspoon black peppercorns, freshly cracked

2 eggs

1 ¼ cups parmesan cheese, grated

1 teaspoon Five-spice powder

Directions

- In a mixing bowl, thoroughly whisk 1 teaspoon of sesame oil, lime juice, wine, tamari sauce, tomato, sambal oelek and garlic.
- Add chicken drumsticks to the marinade and let them sit for 2 hours in the refrigerator.
- Add almond flour, salt, smoked cayenne pepper and black peppercorns to the shallow plate and combine well.
- Whisk the eggs in a separate shallow bowl. Then, mix grated parmesan cheese and Five-spice powder in a third shallow bowl.
- Dip each drumstick into the almond flour mixture, then, dip into eggs and lastly, coat with parmesan mixture on all sides.
- Preheat your Air Fryer to 380 degrees F.
- Air-fry the chicken drumsticks for 25 minutes, flipping them over halfway through. Serve right away!

6. Juicy Marinated Chicken Legs
(Ready in about 45 minutes + marinating time | Servings 6)

Use a food thermometer to check these chicken legs for doneness. Keep in mind that the minimum internal temperature should reach 165 degrees F or higher.

Per serving: 278 Calories; 12.1g Fat; 2.3g Carbs; 33.1g Protein; 1g Sugars

Ingredients

1 ½ tablespoons olive oil

1 teaspoon paprika

1 teaspoon ground cumin

1 teaspoon sea salt

1/2 teaspoon ground black pepper

1/2 teaspoon ground bay leaf

2 garlic cloves, minced

1 cup dry red wine

1 tablespoon Worcestershire sauce

1 teaspoon fresh ginger, grated

1 ½ pounds chicken legs

Directions

- Combine olive oil, paprika, cumin, sea salt, black pepper, ground bay leaf, garlic, wine, Worcestershire sauce, and ginger in a saucepan.
- Bring the mixture to a rolling boil for 1 to 2 minutes; then, reduce heat and simmer for a further 10 minutes, stirring periodically.
- Allow the marinade to cool; now, marinate chicken legs overnight. Next, pat them dry.
- Brush the sides and bottom of a cooking basket with oil.
- Cook the marinated chicken legs at 380 degrees for 35 minutes, flipping them over half-way through. Serve with a salad of choice.

7. Turkey Burgers with Mustard Sauce

(Ready in about 15 minutes | Servings 6)

Prepare fried burgers without excess oil! This ultimate comfort food has never been easier to prepare! Serve with a tangy mustard sauce to make your burgers taste even better.

Per serving: 209 Calories; 12.4g Fat; 0.8g Carbs; 23.2g Protein; 0.2g Sugars

Ingredients

1 ½ pounds ground turkey
1/4 teaspoon ground marjoram
A pinch of grated nutmeg
1/2 teaspoon cayenne pepper
1 teaspoon flaky sea salt
1/4 teaspoon black pepper, preferably
   freshly ground

For the Mustard Sauce:
2 tablespoons erythritol
2 tablespoons sour cream
1/4 cup mayonnaise
2 tablespoons Dijon mustard

Directions

- Begin by preheating your Air Fryer to 330 degrees F. Thoroughly combine ground turkey with marjoram, nutmeg, cayenne pepper, salt and ground black pepper.
- Shape the mixture into 6 burgers.
- Spritz a cooking basket with a nonstick cooking spray. Cook the burgers for 8 to 12 minutes or to the desired degree of doneness.
- Meanwhile, whisk all of the ingredients for the mustard sauce. Serve warm burgers with the prepared sauce and burger buns. Bon appétit!

8. Fried Teriyaki Turkey Strips

(Ready in about 15 minutes + marinating time | Servings 8)

Here's a fantastic way to get the taste of turkey tenders without extra calories! The recipe calls for apple sider vinegar but you can use rice vinegar as well.

Per serving: 269 Calories; 13.9g Fat; 4.2g Carbs; 29.7g Protein; 1.4g Sugars

Ingredients

2 tablespoons soy sauce

2 tablespoons apple cider vinegar

1/4 cup erythritol

1 tablespoon olive oil

1 onion, chopped

2 cloves garlic, smashed

1/2 teaspoon salt

1/2 teaspoon cayenne pepper

2 pounds turkey breasts, cut into strips

2 egg whites, beaten

1 cup parmesan cheese, grated

Directions

- In a mixing dish, thoroughly combine soy sauce, apple cider vinegar, erythritol, olive oil, onion, garlic, salt, and cayenne pepper. Add turkey and let it marinate for 2 hours.
- Pat turkey strips dry and dip them into the egg whites, and finally, dip into parmesan cheese.
- Brush an Air Fryer cooking basket with olive oil.
- Cook at 360 degrees for about 12 minutes or until thoroughly cooked. Serve immediately.

9. Chicken Sausages with Sriracha Mayo

(Ready in about 15 minutes | Servings 4)

Need a last-minute dinner for a family gathering? Serve these juicy sausages with a spicy mayo sauce.

Per serving: 277 Calories; 25.4g Fat; 3.1g Carbs; 8.7g Protein; 1.9g Sugars

Ingredients

4 Italian chicken sausages

For the Sauce:
1/2 cup keto mayonnaise
1 garlic clove, minced
2 tablespoons Sriracha
1/4 teaspoon salt

Directions

- Begin by preheating your Air Fryer to 360 degrees F. Prick holes in the sausages.
- Place the sausages in the cooking basket. Cook about 6 to 7 minutes.
- Turn the sausages and cook another 6 to 7 minutes or until they're thoroughly cooked.
- Meanwhile, make the sauce by whisking mayonnaise, garlic, Sriracha, and salt. Serve with warm sausages over dinner rolls. Bon appétit!

10. Queso Añejo Chicken Ole

(Ready in about 30 minutes | Servings 6)

Tender chicken breasts baked in a spicy sauce and topped with a high-quality Mexican cheese. This dish is elegant and sophisticated but so fun and easy to prepare.

Per serving: 322 Calories; 16.3g Fat; 3g Carbs; 38.9g Protein; 1.5g Sugars

Ingredients

2 tablespoons sesame oil

Salt and ground black pepper, to taste

10 ounces salsa

1 ½ pounds chicken breasts

1 cup Queso Añejo, shredded

Directions

- Begin by preheating your Air Fryer to 380 degrees F.
- To make the sauce, mix the sesame oil, salt, black pepper, and salsa in a bowl.
- Arrange the chicken in a baking dish. Pour the sauce over them.
- Cook for 15 minutes, turning halfway through. Afterwards, top chicken with shredded cheese and bake an additional 10 minutes. Bon appétit!

11. Taco Chicken Drumsticks with Vegetables

(Ready in about 40 minutes | Servings 6)

Make these chicken drumsticks when you want to surprise your family with an elegant and tasty meal. In addition, chicken drumsticks are economical and practical. Win-win!

Per serving: 280 Calories; 10.1g Fat; 8.2g Carbs; 37.6g Protein; 4.8g Sugars

Ingredients

1 ½ pounds chicken drumsticks

1 tablespoon Taco seasoning mix

2 carrots, cut into matchsticks

1 green bell pepper, sliced

1 red bell pepper, sliced

1 yellow onion, clicked

1 teaspoon sea salt

1/2 teaspoon ground black pepper

1/2 teaspoon red pepper flakes, crushed

1 tablespoon olive oil

Directions

- Start by preheating your Air Fryer to 370 degrees F.
- Coat a cooking basket of your Air Fryer with a piece of aluminum foil. Add chicken drumsticks and sprinkle them with Taco seasoning mix.
- Cook for 20 minutes, flipping them halfway through. Then, reserve chicken drumsticks, keeping them warm.
- Toss the vegetable with salt, black pepper, and red pepper; drizzle them with olive oil and set your Air Fryer to cook at 380 degrees F.
- Cook the vegetables for 15 minutes. Add the prepared chicken back to the Air Fryer and cook an additional 5 minutes.
- Transfer the chicken with vegetables to a serving platter and eat warm. Bon appétit!

12. Family Cheesy Chicken Casserole
(Ready in about 20 minutes | Servings 4)

Loaded with tender chicken breasts, vegetables, and stringy, melty Colby cheese, this casserole is just as good with a family dinner, as it is served on holidays.

Per serving: 556 Calories; 38.5g Fat; 6.2g Carbs; 45.5g Protein; 2.2g Sugars

Ingredients

1 pound chicken breasts, cut into strips

1 teaspoon ground cumin

1 teaspoon chipotle powder

1/2 teaspoon garlic powder

1 teaspoon shallot powder

1 teaspoon porcini powder

1/2 teaspoon flaky sea salt

1 teaspoon mixed whole peppercorns

1/2 cup Romano cheese, grated

1 cup ripe tomatoes, chopped

1 bell pepper, deveined and sliced

1 yellow onion, sliced

10 ounces Colby cheese, shredded

2 tablespoons fresh parsley, chopped

Directions

- Preheat your Air Fryer to 360 degrees F.
- Toss the chicken with ground cumin, chipotle powder, garlic powder, shallot powder, porcini powder, and flaky sea salt.
- Coat a cooking basket with a piece of foil. Place the chicken in the cooking basket; add mixed peppercorns and Romano cheese.
- Add tomatoes, bell pepper, and onion. Top with shredded Colby cheese. Bake for 12 minutes or until thoroughly cooked.
- Sprinkle fresh parsley on top and serve warm. Bon appétit!

13. Thanksgiving Bacon Wrapped Meatloaf

(Ready in about 35 minutes | Servings 4)

Here's one of the best Thanksgiving meatloaves! A bacon is a must in this recipe because the ground turkey tends to dry out in the Air Fryer. Make sure to use a slab bacon or side bacon.
Per serving: 416 Calories; 25.7g Fat; 5.7g Carbs; 43.6g Protein; 1.3g Sugars

Ingredients

1 pound ground turkey
1 egg, beaten
1/4 cup saltine crackers, crushed
1 cup yellow onions, chopped
2 garlic cloves, finely minced
1 teaspoon Dijon mustard
1/4 teaspoon hot red pepper sauce

1/3 cup minced parsley
1 teaspoon dried rosemary
1/2 teaspoon dried oregano
1 teaspoon dried basil
Sea salt and ground black pepper, to
   taste
4 ounces bacon, thin-sliced

Directions

- Begin by preheating your Air Fryer to 380 degrees F. Lien a cooking basket with a sheet of foil.
- Thoroughly combine the ground turkey, egg, saltine crackers, yellow onions, garlic, mustard, hot red pepper sauce, and minced parsley. Season with rosemary, oregano, basil, salt, and ground black pepper.
- Shape the mixture into a loaf with wet hands and place in the cooking basket. Brush the meatloaf with oil. Now, place the slices of bacon crosswise over loaf. Make sure to overlap them slightly.
- Bake for 30 minutes or until a meat thermometer registers 160 degrees F.
- Allow the meatloaf to stand for a couple of minutes before slicing. Serve warm with mashed potatoes.

14. Turkey Bacon with Broccoli
(Ready in about 20 minutes | Servings 6)

This turkey bacon tastes so divine! Best of all, you only need 20 minutes to get your dinner ready!

Per serving: 403 Calories; 36.2g Fat; 2.6g Carbs; 16.8g Protein; 0.3g Sugars

Ingredients

1 pound turkey bacon, sliced

1 pound broccoli, broken into florets

2 garlic cloves, minced

1/2 teaspoon flaky sea salt

1/3 teaspoon ground black pepper

1/3 teaspoon red pepper flakes

1/4 teaspoon dried dill weed

1 tablespoon olive oil

Directions

- Begin by preheating your Air Fryer to 390 degrees F.
- Place the slices of bacon in the pan and insert it into your Air Fryer. Cook for 8 minutes. Reserve.
- Toss broccoli with garlic, sea salt, black pepper, red pepper, and dill; drizzle with olive oil. Now, preheat your Air Fryer to 400 degrees F.
- Cook for 8 minutes. Serve cooked bacon with broccoli. Bon appétit!

PORK

15. Easy Pork Cutlets with Enchilada Sauce
(Ready in about 25 minutes | Servings 4)

These pork cutlets are tender and delicious. Make a big batch of enchilada sauce because you can freeze leftovers for later.

Per serving: 496 Calories; 27.8g Fat; 5.5g Carbs; 53.4g Protein; 1.9g Sugars

Ingredients

4 pork cutlets
1 egg white
Salt and ground black pepper, to taste
1 teaspoon red pepper flakes, crushed
1/2 cup Parmesan cheese, grated
1/2 cup pork rinds

For Enchilada Sauce:
1 tablespoon olive oil
1 tablespoon flaxseed meal
1 large-sized tomato, chopped
1/2 teaspoon erythritol
1/2 teaspoon chili powder
1/2 teaspoon garlic powder
1/2 teaspoon shallot powder
Kosher salt and freshly ground black pepper, to taste

Directions

- Preheat your Air Fryer to 380 degrees F.
- In a mixing bowl, whisk the egg white together with salt, black pepper, and red pepper flakes.
- Dip pork cutlets in the egg mixture. Then, coat pork cutlets with parmesan and pork rinds. Cook for 15 minutes.
- Meanwhile, heat the olive oil in a pan that is preheated over a moderate heat. Gradually add flaxseed meal and stir to combine for 2 minutes.
- Add the remaining ingredients for the sauce, bringing it to a boil; then, turn the heat to a medium-low; simmer an additional 8 minutes.
- Serve over pork cutlets. Enjoy!

16. Festive Roasted Pork Belly

(Ready in about 3 hours | Servings 6)

Choosing the right pork belly is half way to success. Use a pork belly with a thick skin for the crispy and flavorful pork roast. Happy air-frying!

Per serving: 623 Calories; 62.4g Fat; 3.8g Carbs; 10.8g Protein; 3.1g Sugars

Ingredients

1 ½ pounds pork belly
1 ½ tablespoons oyster sauce
1 teaspoon stone grain mustard
1/2 teaspoon hot red pepper sauce
2 tablespoons tamari sauce
2 tablespoons Shaoxing rice wine

1 tablespoon olive oil
1 tablespoon raw honey
1/2 teaspoon dried thyme
1/2 teaspoon dried oregano
1/2 teaspoon flaky sea salt
1/2 teaspoon ground black pepper

Directions

- Blanch pork belly in a large pot of boiling water approximately 15 minutes. Now, pricks the skin with a steel skewer.
- Place the pork in a mixing bowl. Add the remaining ingredients and toss to coat on all sides. Place the pork in your refrigerator and let it stand at least 2 hours.
- Then, preheat your Air Fryer to 380 degrees F. Cook the marinated pork for 12 minutes.
- Turn the temperature to 330 degrees and cook for another 25 minutes, basting with the remaining marinade.
- Serve warm with baked potatoes. Bon appétit!

17. Tortilla Chip-Crusted Pork

(Ready in about 20 minutes | Servings 8)

If you are a great believer in a tradition of family dinner, this is the right recipe for you. You can experiment with this recipe and add Romano cheese. Enjoy!

Per serving: 388 Calories; 25.9g Fat; 2.1g Carbs; 34.2g Protein; 0.2g Sugars

Ingredients

2 pounds pork shoulder, sliced 3/4-inch thick

1 teaspoon salt

1/4 teaspoon ground black pepper

2 eggs, whisked

1 cup Parmesan cheese, grated

1/4 teaspoon cayenne pepper

1 teaspoon garlic powder

1/2 teaspoon chipotle powder

Directions

- Begin by preheating your Air Fryer to 390 degrees F; now, spritz the cooking basket with a nonstick spray.
- Sprinkle each piece of pork with salt and black pepper. Add the eggs in a shallow bowl.
- Combine crushed tortilla chips, cayenne pepper, garlic powder, and chipotle powder in another shallow bowl.
- Dip each piece of pork in the eggs, then, tortilla chips mixture.
- Cook for 15 minutes, flipping once or twice; work in batches to ensure even cooking. Eat warm with coleslaw

18. Herbed Pork Sausage Meatballs

(Ready in about 20 minutes | Servings 4)

Making sausage meatballs takes only a few minutes. The result is an amazing bowl of comfort food.

Per serving: 179 Calories; 7.8g Fat; 4.8g Carbs; 22.4g Protein; 2g Sugars

Ingredients

3/4 pound pork sausage (bangers)

1/4 pound ground beef

1 leek, finely chopped

2 garlic cloves, finely minced

1 teaspoon dried thyme

1 teaspoon dried rosemary

1/2 teaspoon dried oregano

1 ½ teaspoons whole grain mustard

Salt and ground black pepper, to taste

Directions

- Preheat your Air Fryer to 380 degrees F.
- Cut the sausage and squeeze out the sausage meat. Add to a large-sized bowl. Add the other ingredients and mix to combine well.
- Shape the sausage mixture into meatballs with damp hands.
- Cook for 13 to 16 minutes, shaking occasionally. Serve over warm polenta and enjoy!

19. BBQ Pork Ribs

(Ready in about 30 minutes | Servings 4)

If you are looking for the quickest way to grill pork ribs, look no further. Use the Air Fryer, your little kitchen helper.

Per serving: 161 Calories; 6.4g Fat; 0.5g Carbs; 23.6g Protein; 0g Sugars

Ingredients

1 pound pork ribs, cut into 2 sections
2 garlic cloves, halved
1/2 teaspoon salt
1/4 teaspoon red pepper flakes, crushed

Freshly ground black pepper, to your
   liking
1/2 teaspoon liquid smoke

Directions

- Blanch pork ribs in a pot of a lightly-salted boiling water. Drain pork ribs and dry them with kitchen towels.
- Rub pork ribs with garlic halves. Season with salt, red pepper flakes, and ground black pepper.
- Lastly, drizzle with liquid smoke.
- Cook in the preheated Air Fryer at 380 degrees F for 25 minutes. Bon appétit!

20. Roast Pork Tenderloin with Chimichurri Sauce
(Ready in about 40 minutes | Servings 6)

Buttery tenderloin with a zingy Chimichurri sauce might become your new favorite! You can use fresh cilantro, ground cumin and red chili for the sauce as well.

Per serving: 224 Calories; 9.8g Fat; 2.5g Carbs; 30g Protein; 1g Sugars

Ingredients

1 ½ pounds pork tenderloin
1 ½ tablespoons butter, at room temperature
1/4 teaspoon ground black pepper
Flaky sea salt, to taste

For Chimichurri Sauce:
2 tablespoons fresh parsley, chopped
2 garlic cloves, very finely chopped
1 onion, chopped
3 tablespoons extra-virgin olive oil
1/2 teaspoon dried crushed red pepper
1 ½ tablespoons wine vinegar

Directions

- Start by preheating your Air Fryer to 370 degrees F. Rub pork tenderloins with softened butter; season with black pepper and sea salt.
- Cook for 25 minutes. Decrease the temperature to 360 degrees F, flip the pork tenderloins and cook on the other side for 12 minutes more.
- Meanwhile, whisk all ingredients for the sauce. Serve with warm pork tenderloin. Bon appétit!

21. Pork and Pancetta Meatloaf
(Ready in about 35 minutes | Servings 6)

This juicy meatloaf will be gone as soon as it hits the table. However, that's the point, isn't it?
Per serving: 323 Calories; 20.1g Fat; 4.7g Carbs; 29.3g Protein; 2.4g Sugars

Ingredients

For the Meatloaf:
1 pound ground pork
1/4 pounds pancetta, chopped
2 teaspoons Provençal herbs
1 egg, beaten
1/2 cup pork rind
1 cup white onion, chopped
2 garlic cloves, minced
Kosher salt and freshly ground pepper,
    to taste
1 teaspoon smoked paprika
1/4 teaspoon dried oregano
1 teaspoon dried sage, crushed

For the Sauce:
1 cup tomato sauce, canned, no salt
    added
1 teaspoon erythritol
1/2 teaspoon ground black pepper
1/4 teaspoon mustard powder
1/8 teaspoon grated nutmeg

Directions

- Start by preheating your Air Fryer to 390 degrees F.
- Combine all ingredients for the meatloaf in a mixing dish. Transfer to a baking pan and shape into a loaf.
- Mix all ingredients for the sauce. Pour the sauce over the meatloaf. Put the baking pan into an Air Fryer cooking basket. Bake 30 minutes in the preheated Air Fryer.
- Allow your meatloaf to cool slightly before serving. Enjoy!

22. Bubble & Squeak with Ham and Feta

(Ready in about 35 minutes | Servings 3)

Here's the recipe for one of the most economical dishes in the world. You can use any leftover vegetables, mashed potatoes, veggie stuffing, and so forth.

Per serving: 317 Calories; 21.3g Fat; 6.5g Carbs; 24.4g Protein; 3.1g Sugars

Ingredients

4 eggs

6 slices of ham, chopped

1 cup Brussels sprouts, chopped

1/2 yellow onion, chopped

1/2 cup feta cheese, crumbled

1 teaspoon dried basil

1/2 teaspoon dried dill weed

1/2 teaspoon sea salt

1/4 teaspoon black pepper, preferably freshly ground

Directions

- Whisk the eggs in a medium-sized mixing dish. Add the chopped ham, Brussels sprouts, and onions.
- Stir in the cheese; stir to combine well. Season with dried basil, dill, salt and black pepper; spoon the mixture into a baking pan.
- Place in the cooking basket of your Air Fryer.
- Bake for 30 minutes at 360 degrees F. Serve warm and enjoy!

23. Fried Bacon with Rutabaga Fries

(Ready in about 1 hour | Servings 4)

This country-style dish makes a perfect family lunch. Mmm, smells good!
Per serving: 344 Calories; 29.6g Fat; 9.1g Carbs; 9.9g Protein; 6.4g Sugars

Ingredients

8 rashes pork bacon

1 pound rutabaga, peeled and cut sticks

2 teaspoons olive oil

Flaky sea salt and black pepper, to taste

1/2 teaspoon cayenne pepper

1 teaspoon rosemary

1 teaspoon marjoram

1 teaspoon basil

1 teaspoon garlic powder

Directions

- Preheat your Air Fryer to 400 degrees F. Arrange the rashes of pork bacon in the cooking basket.
- Now, cook the bacon for 8 minutes or to your desired doneness; reserve.
- Meanwhile, place rutabaga in a bowl of cold water and let them soak for 35 minutes. Pat them dry with a kitchen towel.
- Toss rutabaga with olive oil, salt, black pepper, cayenne pepper, rosemary, marjoram, basil, and garlic powder until they are well coated.
- Cook the seasoned rutabaga for 18 minutes at 400 degrees F. Check for doneness and top with reserved bacon.
- Cook for 1 minute more at 370 degrees F or until thoroughly cooked. Bon appétit!

24. Easy Pork Chops with Onion

(Ready in about 20 minutes | Servings 5)

Are you searching for a perfect pork chop recipe? Your mission is over. These pork chops are easy and fun to make and they'll shake up the routine at family dinner time.

Per serving: 273 Calories; 9.1g Fat; 2.5g Carbs; 42.7g Protein; 0.9g Sugars

Ingredients

5 bone-in pork chops, trimmed of fat

2 garlic cloves, halved

2 tablespoons whole grain mustard

Se salt and ground black pepper, to
taste

1 teaspoon paprika

1 onion, cut into 5 thick slices

Directions

- Start by preheating your Air Fryer to 400 degrees F.
- Rub pork chops with garlic halves and mustard on both sides. Sprinkle with salt, black pepper, and paprika.
- Arrange pork chops in the cooking basket. Cook for 5 minutes. Then, turn over and cook another 4 minutes.
- Place a slice of onion on each pork chop and continue to cook an additional 4 minutes. Serve warm with refreshing cucumber and yogurt salad. Bon appétit!

25. Boston Butt with Sherry Wine Sauce

(Ready in about 1 hour 10 minutes | Servings 8)

Pork roast with a restaurant-caliber sauce. Boston but gets a flavor boost from sherry wine and dried Mexican oregano.

Per serving: 352 Calories; 24.1g Fat; 1.7g Carbs; 30.1g Protein; 0.6g Sugars

Ingredients

2 pounds Boston butt

1 ½ tablespoons olive oil

1/2 cup onions, minced

1 teaspoon salt

1/2 teaspoon ground black pepper

1 teaspoon dried Mexican oregano

2 garlic cloves, minced

2 tablespoons fresh coriander, chopped

1 teaspoon chili pepper, minced

1/2 cup dry white wine

Directions

- Make shallow cuts on the meat by using a sharp knife. Add the remaining ingredients and marinate the meat overnight.
- Preheat your Air Fryer to 350 degrees F for 5 to 10 minutes. Cook marinated Boston butt for 55 minutes, turning halfway through cooking time.
- In the meantime, make the sauce. Cook the marinade in a pan over medium-high until reduced by half.
- Slice prepared Boston butt and serve with the sauce on the side. Bon appétit!

26. The Best Pork Sliders Ever

(Ready in about 25 minutes | Servings 6)

Pork sliders are endlessly inspiring to home chefs. Use a mixture of beef and pork mince for even better results. Mix in chopped salami or cooked, crushed bacon. Or simply experiment with your favorite combo of seasonings.

Per serving: 480 Calories; 33g Fat; 6g Carbs; 38.1g Protein; 3.7g Sugars

Ingredients

1 ½ pounds ground pork
1 teaspoon Swiss vegetable bouillon
   powder
2 teaspoon Shoyu sauce
2 green onions, chopped
1 teaspoon garlic paste
1 teaspoon shallot powder
1 teaspoon chipotle powder
Salt and ground black pepper, to taste
1 ½ teaspoons dried parsley flakes
6 slices Cheddar cheese

For the slider buns:

1/4 cup mozzarella cheese, grated
3 ounces cream cheese
2 eggs
1 3/4 cup almond flour
1 teaspoon baking powder

Directions

- Mix ground pork, bouillon powder, Shoyu sauce, green onions, garlic paste, shallot powder, chipotle powder, salt, ground black pepper, and parsley in a large bowl.
- Shape the meat mixture into 6 patties with oiled hands; transfer to a cooking basket.
- Cook in the preheated your Air Fryer at 390 degrees F for 20 minutes; work in batches.
- To make keto slider buns, mix dry ingredients for the buns; then, mix wet ingredients. Add wet mixture to dry mixture; mix to combine well.
- Preheat your oven to 400 degrees F; place a rack in the middle of the oven. Line a baking sheet with parchment paper. Bake your buns for 12 minutes or until the outside has browned.
- Place one slice of cheese on each patty and serve with slider buns.

27. Garam Masala and Orange Pork

(Ready in about 3 hours 30 minutes | Servings 6)

Try this exotic pork recipe for the next dinner party. It is important to marinate pork ribs at least 3 hours to make them easier to eat.

Per serving: 288 Calories; 16.2g Fat; 3g Carbs; 30.7g Protein; 1.9g Sugars

Ingredients

1 ½ pounds baby back ribs

Sea salt and ground black pepper, to
   taste

1 teaspoon fresh ginger root, minced

1 teaspoon garam masala spice

1/2 cup fresh orange juice

1/4 cup soy sauce

1 tablespoon olive oil

1/4 cup fresh cilantro, chopped

Directions

- Discard the membranes from the back of pork ribs; cut pork ribs into 3 to 4 pieces.
- Toss baby back ribs with salt, pepper, ginger, garam masala, orange juice, soy sauce, and olive oil. Transfer to the refrigerator and let it marinate for 3 hours.
- Preheat your Air Fryer to 360 degrees F. Discard the marinade and place pork ribs in the cooking basket. Cook for 13 minutes.
- Turn and cook for 16 minutes on the other side.
- Meanwhile, cook the marinade in a saucepan over a moderate flame; cook until the sauce is reduced by half and slightly thickened.
- Pour the sauce over pork ribs, garnish with fresh cilantro and serve warm.

28. Spicy Habanero Pork Filet Mignon

(Ready in about 3 hours 20 minutes | Servings 4)

The filet mignon is a part of the loin cut. This is a lean cut and it should be tenderized or marinated for a while.

Per serving: 420 Calories; 24.2g Fat; 5.9g Carbs; 42.7g Protein; 2.9g Sugars

Ingredients

4 (4-ounce) pork fillets
2 garlic cloves, pressed
1/2 white onion, chopped
1 teaspoon Dijon mustard
1 teaspoon fresh ginger root, grated
1 bell pepper, chopped

1 Habanero pepper, chopped
Salt and black pepper, to taste
2 tablespoons soy sauce
2 tablespoons champagne vinegar
1 ½ tablespoons sesame oil

Directions

- Place the pork filets in a re-sealable zipper storage bag. Add the remaining ingredients and shake vigorously to combine.
- Place in the refrigerator and allow it to marinate for 3 hours.
- Preheat your Air Fryer to 380 degrees F. Cook for 15 minutes, flipping once. Serve with mashed potatoes and beet root salad.

BEEF

29. Bologna Sausage with Mushrooms and Peppers

(Ready in about 25 minutes | Servings 4)

Here's an easy, economical and satisfying recipe that you will love. Bologna is flavorful on its own but you can add sautéed vegetables to take it to the next level of deliciousness!

Per serving: 310 Calories; 26.4g Fat; 6.4g Carbs; 12g Protein; 2.3g Sugars

Ingredients

6 ounces Bologna sausages

1 ½ tablespoons Dijon mustard

1 tablespoon olive oil

1 cup button mushrooms, sliced

1/2 white onion, chopped

1 red bell pepper, sliced

1 green bell pepper, sliced

1/2 teaspoon garlic powder

1/2 teaspoon cayenne pepper

Salt and black pepper, to taste

Directions

- Preheat your Air Fryer to 380 degrees for about 4 minutes.
- Cook the sausages for 7 minutes; turn them over and cook an additional 7 minutes; top with mustard and reserve.
- Meanwhile, heat the oil in a sauté pan that is preheated over a moderately high heat. Sauté the mushrooms with onions and bell peppers,
- Season with garlic powder, cayenne powder, salt, and black pepper and stir to combine. Transfer to a serving platter along with reserved sausages.
- Serve with dinner rolls. Bon appétit!

30. Ranchero and Scallion Burgers
(Ready in about 35 minutes | Servings 4)

Who doesn't love burgers? These fantastic burgers can be done so easily in the Air Fryer. For the best results, use 80% lean ground chuck.

Per serving: 405 Calories; 23.8g Fat; 8.9g Carbs; 40.1g Protein; 2.4g Sugars

Ingredients

1 1/3 pounds ground chuck
2 garlic cloves, minced
1 jalapeño pepper, finely minced
1/2 cup scallions, peeled and chopped
Salt and ground black pepper, to taste
1 tablespoon tomato puree
1/4 cup Parmesan cheese, grated
1/2 cup iceberg lettuce, shredded
1/2 cup chunky salsa

For the keto rolls:
1 cup almond flour
1/4 cup coconut flour
1/3 cup psyllium husks
1/4 packed cup flax seed meal
1 teaspoon cream of tartar
1/2 teaspoon baking soda
1 teaspoon garlic powder
A pinch of salt
1 tablespoon caraway seeds
4 eggs
1 cup water, lukewarm

Directions

- Preheat your Air Fryer to 390 degrees F.
- In a mixing bowl, thoroughly combine ground chuck with garlic, jalapeño pepper, scallions, salt, black pepper, tomato puree, and cheese.
- Form this meat mixture into 4 patties. Bake for 25 minutes.
- To make the keto rolls, in a mixing bowl, thoroughly combine flour, psyllium husks, flax seed meal. Add cream of tartar and baking soda.
- Now, stir in the garlic powder, salt, and caraway seeds.
- Now, fold in eggs and mix to combine. Gradually pour in the water and mix again. Make the buns using a spoon; place them on a baking sheet that is lined with a parchment paper.
- Bake in the preheated oven at 350 degrees F for about 45 minutes.
- Serve the prepared patties over the keto rolls, garnished with iceberg lettuce and chunky salsa. Bon appétit!

31. Mint and Cilantro Chuck

(Ready in about 20 minutes + marinating time | Servings 4)

Cooking complete meals to perfection has never been easier. The Air Fryer is a revolutionary kitchen appliance that makes everything better!

Per serving: 436 Calories; 34.4g Fat; 1.6g Carbs; 28.6g Protein; 0.1g Sugars

Ingredients

- 1 ¼ pounds chuck, cut into four portions
- 1 teaspoon salt
- 1/2 teaspoon ground black pepper
- 1/2 teaspoon cayenne pepper
- 1/4 cup fresh cilantro, finely chopped
- 1/4 cup mint, finely minced
- 4 garlic cloves, finely minced
- 1 teaspoon cayenne pepper
- 1 teaspoon ground cumin
- 2 tablespoons olive oil
- 3 tablespoons champagne vinegar

Directions

- In a mixing dish, combine chuck with the other ingredients; wrap with foil. Transfer the dish to your refrigerator; let it marinate at least 2 hours,
- Preheat your Air Fryer to 400 degrees F for 5 minutes
- Discard the marinade and place the chuck on a double layer rack in your Air Fryer. Cook for 12 minutes, flipping once. Bon appétit!

32. Flank Steak with Roasted Garlic Sauce

(Ready in about 40 minutes + marinating time | Servings 5)

How do you know when your steak is done? The easiest way is to use a meat thermometer. Here are the recommended temperatures: 130 degrees F for rare, 155 degrees F for medium and 165 degrees F for well done.

Per serving: 390 Calories; 24.6g Fat; 6.8g Carbs; 33.8g Protein; 3.3g Sugars

Ingredients

1 ½ pounds flank steak
2 tablespoons sesame oil
1/4 cup soy sauce
2 tablespoons xylitol
2 tablespoons red wine vinegar
1 tablespoon fresh chives, chopped
1 teaspoon basil
1 teaspoon oregano
1/2 teaspoon hot pepper sauce
Salt and freshly ground black pepper,
    to taste
1 garlic bulb, peeled

For the Sauce:
2 tablespoons butter
1/2 cup whipping cream
1 ½ tablespoons flaxseed meal
1/2 cup Parmesan cheese, shredded

Directions

- Start by preheating the Air Fryer to 390 degrees F for 5 to 10 minutes. Spritz a cooking basket with a nonstick cooking spray and roast the garlic for 10 minutes; reserve.
- In a mixing dish, combine flank steak with sesame oil, soy sauce, xylitol, vinegar, chives, basil, oregano, hot pepper sauce, salt, and black pepper.
- Transfer the dish to your refrigerator and marinate it for at least 3 hours and up to overnight.
- Now, preheat the Air Fryer to 400 degrees F. Roast the flank steak for 12 minutes.
- Squeeze pulp from garlic cloves. Cook garlic, butter, whipping cream, and flaxseed meal in a pan over medium-high heat, stirring frequently.
- Cook until the sauce is thickened. Heat off; stir in Parmesan cheese. Serve with prepared flank steak.

33. Delicious Beef Meatballs

(Ready in about 20 minutes | Servings 4)

These balls might become a staple menu item in your kitchen. The Air Fryer is really awesome!

Per serving: 256 Calories; 9.9g Fat; 7.2g Carbs; 35.5g Protein; 4.5g Sugars

Ingredients

1 ½ pounds beef, ground

1 teaspoon Worcestershire sauce

Flaky sea salt and freshly ground black
   pepper, to taste

1 teaspoon paprika

1/2 teaspoon granulated garlic

2 tablespoons scallions, chopped

4 tablespoons ketchup

4 teaspoons mustard

1/2 red onion, chopped

Directions

- In a mixing dish, combine the meat, Worcestershire, salt, black pepper, paprika, granulated garlic, and scallions.
- Shape the mixture into 8 balls. Then, preheat your Air Fryer to 370 degrees F. Cook for 15 minutes, shaking once or twice.
- Divide the sausage balls, ketchup, mustard, pickled cucumbers, and chopped onion among four serving plates. Bon appétit!

34. Family Grilled Beef Sirloin
(Ready in about 25 minutes | Servings 4)

Whether you're an Air Fryer newbie or you are an old hand at air frying, this recipe will amaze you!

Per serving: 266 Calories; 8.8g Fat; 0.5g Carbs; 43.1g Protein; 0g Sugars

Ingredients

1 ¼ pounds beef sirloin, trim off excess fat and silver skin

1 tablespoon cider vinegar

2 garlic cloves, finely minced

1 teaspoon fresh ginger, grated

Sea salt and coarsely ground black pepper, to taste

1/2 teaspoon smoked cayenne pepper

Directions

- Cut beef sirloin into steaks.
- In a small mixing bowl, whisk the vinegar, garlic, ginger, salt, black pepper, and cayenne. Massage this rub mixture into the meat; let it marinate for 2 hours in your refrigerator.
- Preheat your Air Fryer to 400 degrees F for 5 to 10 minutes. Insert the Air Fryer grill pan.
- Place the prepared sirloin on the grill pan.
- Cook for 14 minutes or until a meat thermometer inserted in center of thickest part reaches 160 degrees F. Bon appétit!

35. Herbed Beef Eye Round Roast

(Ready in about 45 minutes + marinating time | Servings 4)

Looking for a surprisingly sensational beef recipe to amaze your guests? Here is a great opportunity to cook beef eye round roast in the Air Fryer. Enjoy!

Per serving: 293 Calories; 12.3g Fat; 0.5g Carbs; 42.5g Protein; 0.1g Sugars

Ingredients

1 tablespoon fresh lime juice
1 ½ tablespoons sesame oil
1/2 teaspoon mustard seeds
1 sprig thyme, leaves picked and
    chopped
2 sprigs rosemary, leaves picked and
    chopped
Salt and coarsely ground black pepper,
    to your liking
1 ½ pounds beef eye round roast, trim
    off excess fat

Directions

- Preheat your Air Fryer to 380 degrees F. Mix fresh lime juice, sesame oil, mustard seeds, thyme, rosemary, salt, and black pepper.
- Massage the rub mix into the beef eye round roast; wrap it in a saran wrap and place in the refrigerator for 2 hours.
- Cook for 45 minutes, flipping halfway through cooking time. Check for doneness and let it rest for a couple of minutes before slicing and serving.
- Cut across the grain and serve. Bon appétit!

36. Sirloin Steaks with Roasted Zucchini

(Ready in about 25 minutes + marinating time | Servings 4)

Here's one of the most popular family dinners – steak with roasted vegetables. Serve with a glass of a good red wine.

Per serving: 371 Calories; 17.1g Fat; 7g Carbs; 47.6g Protein; 2.3g Sugars

Ingredients

4 sirloin steaks

1/4 cup apple cider vinegar

2 tablespoons tamari sauce

1 teaspoon grated ginger

2 tablespoons scallions, chopped

2 garlic cloves, minced

2 tablespoons sesame oil

Salt and ground black pepper, to taste

1 teaspoon paprika

1 pound zucchini, sliced

1 tablespoon olive oil

Directions

- Place sirloin steaks, apple cider vinegar, tamari sauce, grated ginger, scallions, garlic, sesame oil, salt, pepper, and paprika in a mixing dish.
- Wrap with a piece of foil and let it marinate at least 3 hours in the refrigerator.
- Preheat the Air Fryer to 400 degrees F. Cook for 13 minutes, working in batches. Reserve, keeping warm.
- Place zucchini in a cooking basket. Sprinkle the zucchini with salt and pepper to taste; drizzle with olive oil. Cook at 400 degrees F for 12 minutes, shaking halfway through cooking time.
- Serve with sirloin steaks. Bon appétit!

37. Steak Fingers with Pickle Sauce

(Ready in about 20 minutes | Servings 6)

Here's an all-time favorite! These steak fingers go perfectly with tangy pickle sauce for dipping. Kids will be delighted!

Per serving: 411 Calories; 29.8g Fat; 2.5g Carbs; 33.1g Protein; 1.1g Sugars

Ingredients

1/2 cup pork rinds

1/2 cup Romano cheese, grated

1 teaspoon paprika

1 teaspoon thyme

Salt and ground black pepper, to your liking

3/4 cup water

2 eggs

1 ½ pounds cube steak, cut into 1-inch strips

1/2 cup mayo

2 tablespoons sour cream

1 pickled cucumber, finely chopped

1 garlic clove, minced

Directions

- Mix pork rinds with Romano cheese, paprika, thyme, salt, ground black pepper and water in a shallow bowl; add the eggs and mix to combine well.
- Tenderize cube steak by pounding with a mallet.
- Dip the beef pieces into the breadcrumb/egg mixture and coat on all sides.
- Cook at 380 degrees F Cook for 14 minutes, flipping halfway through cooking time.
- Meanwhile, make the sauce by mixing mayo with sour cream, pickled cucumber, and minced garlic. Serve with the prepared beef.

38. Extraordinary Beef Koftas with Cauli Rice
(Ready in about 25 minutes | Servings 4)

Loaded with fresh ground beef, fluffy cauli rice, and extraordinary spices, these traditional koftas are sure to please. Try this low-fat version and enjoy!

Per serving: 175 Calories; 8.9g Fat; 6g Carbs; 18.9g Protein; 1.9g Sugars

Ingredients

2 cups cauliflower florets

3/4 pound ground chuck

1 shallot, finely chopped

2 garlic cloves, finely minced

1 teaspoon brown sugar

1 teaspoon paprika

2 tablespoons flaxseed meal

Sea salt and ground black pepper, to taste

1/2 teaspoon ground cumin

5 saffron threads

1 ½ tablespoons loosely packed fresh continental parsley leaves

Directions

- Pulse the cauliflower in a food processor; process until broken down into rice-size pieces.
- Heat olive oil in a pan; now, cook the cauliflower over medium heat for about 4 minutes or until heated through; fluff the cauli rice with a fork.
- Add the remaining ingredients; mix until everything is well incorporated.
- Now, mound a tablespoonful of the meat mixture around a wooden skewer into a pointed-ended sausage using your hands.
- Cook in the preheated Air Fryer for 25 minutes at 360 degrees F. Serve with French fries and enjoy!

39. Crispy Beef Schnitzel
(Ready in about 20 minutes | Servings 2)

Here's the best beef schnitzel you've ever eaten. You can make homemade buttered crumbs by spreading each slice of toast with soft butter. Then, pulse buttered toast slices in your food processor.

Per serving: 447 Calories; 29.9g Fat; 2.5g Carbs; 42.3g Protein; 0.1g Sugars

Ingredients

2 beef schnitzel

1 paprika, or more to taste

1/2 teaspoon sea salt

1/4 freshly ground black pepper, or
   more to taste

1/3 cup Parmesan cheese, preferably
   freshly grated

2 tablespoons olive oil

1 egg

2 tablespoons fresh cilantro, roughly
   chopped

Directions

- Preheat your Air Fryer to 390 degrees F for 5 to 10 minutes.
- Season beef schnitzels with paprika, salt, and ground black pepper.
- In a shallow dish, combine buttered crumbs with oil. In a separate shallow dish, whisk the egg until pale and frothy.
- Now, coat beef schnitzels with the beaten egg; then, coat it with Parmesan cheese.
- Cook for 12 minutes, flipping halfway through cooking time. Serve warm, garnished with fresh cilantro. Bon appétit!

40. Favorite Family Picadillo
(Ready in about 25 minutes | Servings 4)

Picadillo is a traditional Spanish dish that is similar to stew and hash. You can use it as a stuffing for tacos and empanadas.

Per serving: 249 Calories; 14g Fat; 8.2g Carbs; 23.8g Protein; 4.2g Sugars

Ingredients

1 ½ tablespoons olive oil
1 pound ground chuck
2 bell peppers, chopped
1 onion, chopped
2 garlic cloves, minced
1/4 cup pimento stuffed olives

2 tomatoes, chopped
2 tablespoons alcaparrado
1 teaspoon ground cumin
Coarse salt and ground black pepper to taste

Directions

- Start by preheating your Air Fryer to 380 degrees F.
- Add the olive oil, ground chuck, bell peppers, onion and garlic to the Air Fryer baking pan. Cook for 9 minutes.
- Add the remaining ingredients and cook for a further 15 minutes. Taste, adjust the seasonings, and serve warm.
- Serve over warm rice. Bon appétit!

41. Ribeye with Mustard and Beer Sauce

(Ready in about 20 minutes | Servings 4)

This flavorful ribeye is previously marinated overnight, then, it is cooked in the Air Fryer and served with zingy dark beer sauce. Perfect!

Per serving: 235 Calories; 10.4g Fat; 4.3g Carbs; 26.3g Protein; 0.5g Sugars

Ingredients

1 pound ribeye

2 teaspoons yellow mustard

2 tablespoons onion, minced

2 garlic cloves, minced

1 tablespoon fresh parsley, chopped

1 ¼ cups dark beer

2 tablespoons lemon juice

2 bay leaves

1 ½ tablespoons olive oil

Salt and ground black pepper, to your
   liking

Directions

- Place all ingredients in mixing dish; let it marinate overnight in the refrigerator.
- Discard the marinade.
- Cook ribeye in the preheated Air Fryer at 400 degrees F for 15 minutes.
- In the meantime, cook the marinade in a pan that is preheated over a moderately high heat. You can add 1 tablespoon of flaxseed meal to thicken the sauce.
- Cook until the sauce is reduced by half. Serve rib eye with the sauce on the side. Bon appétit!

42. Lebanese-Style Beef Strips with Horseradish Sauce

(Ready in about 25 minutes | Servings 4)

Stringy, crispy and delicious, these beef strips are both, sophisticated and easy to prepare. They go wonderfully with horseradish sauce.

Per serving: 319 Calories; 13.9g Fat; 7.9g Carbs; 38.4g Protein; 3.6g Sugars

Ingredients

1 pound beef tenderloin, cut into strips
1/2 cup arrowroot powder
1 teaspoon Seven-spice powder
1 cup buttermilk
Kosher salt and ground black pepper,
    to taste

For the Sauce:
1/2 cup sour cream
2 tablespoons grated fresh horseradish
1 teaspoon stone ground mustard
Sea salt and freshly ground black pepper, to taste

Directions

- Pat dry beef and set it aside.
- In a shallow dish, combine arrowroot and Seven-spice powder. Add the buttermilk with salt, and black pepper to another shallow dish.
- Dip beef strips in the arrowroot mixture. Then, dip into the buttermilk mixture; coat them again with arrowroot mixture on all sides.
- Preheat your Air Fryer to 370 degrees F. Grease the inside of a cooking basket using an oil mister. Now, cook the beef for 14 minutes, shaking the cooking basket once or twice.
- Meanwhile, make the horseradish sauce by mixing all of the sauce ingredients.
- Serve warm beef strips with the prepared horseradish sauce on the side. Bon appétit!

FISH & SEAFOOD

43. Easy Sunday Shrimp
(Ready in about 15 minutes | Servings 4)

Here is a simple yet creative shrimp recipe! Serve with your favorite fixings such as fresh mayo-based sauces or tomato ketchup.

Per serving: 330 Calories; 19.8g Fat; 4.1g Carbs; 32.7g Protein; 0.2g Sugars

Ingredients

1 pound shrimp, veins and shells removed and washed

2 tablespoons dry white wine

3 tablespoons good olive oil

Sea salt and freshly ground black pepper

1 teaspoon paprika

2 eggs

1 cup Parmesan cheese, grated

Directions

- Drizzle shrimp with dry white wine and olive oil. Season with salt, pepper, and paprika to taste.
- Beat the eggs in a shallow bowl. Place dried bread flakes in another shallow bowl.
- Dip your shrimp in egg, then, in grated parmesan cheese.
- Now, preheat the Air Fryer to 360 degrees F. Cook the shrimp for 7 minutes, flipping halfway through cooking time.
- Serve over pasta. Bon appétit!

44. Ginger Lime Glazed Salmon Steaks

(Ready in about 15 minutes + marinating time | Servings 4)

Salmon is loaded with omega-3 fatty acids, B vitamins, selenium, potassium, and antioxidants. Keep this recipe in your back pocket.

Per serving: 210 Calories; 11.5g Fat; 1.7g Carbs; 23.4g Protein; 0.5g Sugars

Ingredients

4 (2-inch thick) salmon steaks

1/2 teaspoon fresh ginger, grated

1 tablespoon Worcestershire sauce

2 tablespoons lime juice

1 teaspoon garlic, minced

1 tablespoon sesame oil

1/2 teaspoon smoked cayenne pepper

1/4 teaspoon dried dill

1/2 teaspoon dried rosemary

1/2 teaspoon sea salt

1/4 teaspoon ground black pepper, or more to taste

Directions

- Preheat your Air Fryer to 380 degrees F. Pat dry salmon steaks with a kitchen towel.
- In a mixing dish, combine the remaining ingredients until everything is well whisked. Add salmon steaks and wrap with a piece of foil.
- Transfer to the refrigerator for 2 hours. Discard the marinade and place the salmon steaks in a cooking basket.
- Cook for 12 minutes, flipping halfway through cooking time.
- Meanwhile, cook the marinade in a saucepan that is preheated over a moderate heat. Cook until the sauce is thickened.
- Pour the sauce over the steaks and serve with Waldorf salad. Bon appétit!

45. Easy Aromatic Cod Filets
(Ready in about 20 minutes | Servings 4)

Fish fillets and nacho chips make it easy to give every dish a little something extra. Serve this crumbed fish with your favorite salad.

Per serving: 212 Calories; 12.2g Fat; 2.1g Carbs; 22.1g Protein; 0.9g Sugars

Ingredients

2 eggs

2 tablespoons olive oil

1 cup almond flour

1 teaspoon sumac

1 teaspoon turmeric

Salt and ground black pepper, to your liking

4 cod filets

2 tablespoons fresh mint leaves, chopped

Directions

- Begin by preheating your Air Fryer to 380 degrees F.
- In a shallow bowl, beat the eggs until frothy.
- In another shallow mixing bowl, combine the oil, almond flour, sumac, turmeric, salt, and black pepper.
- Dip each cod fillets into the beaten eggs. Then, coat with nacho chips mixture until they are covered on all sides.
- Transfer to a cooking basket and cook for 10 minutes or until the fish is thoroughly cooked. Serve garnished with fresh mint leaves. Enjoy!

46. Surimi and Ricotta Wontons

(Ready in about 30 minutes | Servings 5)

These air-fried crispy wontons are perfect garnished with a salad of fresh onion, carrots, apples, and crumbled goat cheese.

Per serving: 252 Calories; 19.4g Fat; 4.8g Carbs; 14.2g Protein; 0.8g Sugars

Ingredients

5 ounces Ricotta cheese, at room temperature

2 tablespoons sour cream

2 tablespoons scallions, chopped

1 teaspoon oyster sauce

5 sticks of surimi, chopped up

1/3 teaspoon sea salt

Lemon pepper, to taste

10 pieces chicken skin

Directions

- Blitz Ricotta, sour cream, scallion, and oyster sauce in your food processor. Transfer to a mixing bowl.
- Add surimi, salt, and lemon pepper to taste; mix to combine.
- Divide the mixture among chicken skin wonton wrappers. Cook in the preheated Air Fryer at 390 degrees F for 10 minutes; work in batches.
- Transfer to a serving platter and serve with a dipping sauce of choice. Bon appétit!

47. King Prawns alla Parmigiana

(Ready in about 15 minutes | Servings 4)

Try these parmesan crusted king prawns that are fried to golden perfection. You won't be disappointed.

Per serving: 225 Calories; 8.6g Fat; 6.6g Carbs; 28.8g Protein; 0.5g Sugars

Ingredients

3/4 cup almond flour

2 egg whites

1 cup Parmigiano-Reggiano, grated

1/2 teaspoon sea salt

1/2 teaspoon ground black pepper

1 teaspoon garlic powder

1/2 teaspoon shallot powder

1/2 teaspoon dried rosemary

1 pound king prawns

1 fresh lemon, cut into wedges

Directions

- To make a breading station, place the flour in a shallow dish. In a separate dish, beat the egg whites.
- In the third dish, place Parmigiano-Reggiano. Add the seasonings and mix to combine well.
- Dip prawns in the flour, then into the egg whites; lastly, dip them in the parmesan mixture until they are covered on all sides.
- Preheat your Air Fryer to 390 degrees F and cook your prawns for 5 to 7 minutes or until golden brown. Serve with lemon wedges and enjoy!

48. Smoked Haddock Fish Cakes
(Ready in about 15 minutes | Servings 6)

The cooler the ingredients are when you shape the patties, the easier it will be to make your fish cakes. You can place the mixture in the refrigerator for 1 to 2 hours before making the patties.

Per serving: 245 Calories; 15.7g Fat; 5.5g Carbs; 21.4g Protein; 1.5g Sugars

Ingredients

1 pound smoked haddock, cooked

1/2 cup cauliflower rice

3 spring onions, finely chopped

1 handful of cheddar cheese, grated

2 tablespoons fresh parsley leaves, chopped

Sea salt and ground black pepper, to taste

1 teaspoon lemon zest

1 cup almond flour

Directions

- Flake the smoked haddock in a mixing bowl. Add the cauli rice, spring onions, cheddar, parsley, salt, pepper and lemon zest.
- Mix until everything is well combined, avoiding breaking up the haddock too much.
- Form the mixture into 6 patties and coat with almond flour on all sides.
- Now, preheat your Air Fryer to 370 degrees F. Transfer the fish cakes to a cooking basket and spritz them with a nonstick cooking spray.
- Cook for 6 minutes or until they're cooked through. Bon appétit!

49. Tilapia Fillets with Sour Cream Sauce

(Ready in about 20 minutes | Servings 4)

Don't be fooled by the simplicity of this fish recipe. This is one of the best recipes for fish fillets you will ever find!

Per serving: 310 Calories; 14.1g Fat; 8.6g Carbs; 36.5g Protein; 0.8g Sugars

Ingredients

2 eggs

1/2 cup crushed tortilla chips

1/2 teaspoon fresh ginger, grated

2 tablespoons fresh cilantro, chopped

1/2 teaspoon sea salt

1/3 teaspoon ground black pepper, to taste

1/2 teaspoon smoked paprika

1/2 teaspoon chipotle powder

4 tilapia fillets

1/2 cup sour cream

2 tablespoons full-fat mayonnaise

1 teaspoon lemon juice

1/2 teaspoon dried dill weed

Directions

- Place the eggs in a shallow bowl and whisk until they are frothy.
- In another mixing bowl, place crushed tortilla chips, ginger, cilantro, salt, black pepper, paprika, and chipotle powder.
- Dip tilapia fillets in the beaten eggs, and then, in the tortilla chips mixture. Cook in the preheated Air Fryer at 380 degrees F for 13 minutes.
- Thoroughly combine sour cream, mayonnaise, lemon juice, and dill weed. Serve with tilapia fillets. Bon appétit!

50. Last Minute Cod Fillets

(Ready in about 15 minutes + marinating time | Servings 4)

This is an extremely simple recipe, perfect for any occasion. You can use other seasonings such as fresh mint, basil or marjoram if you'd like.

Per serving: 156 Calories; 7.3g Fat; 4.1g Carbs; 18.4g Protein; 1.5g Sugars

Ingredients

4 cod fillets

1/2 teaspoon seasoned salt

1/2 teaspoon white pepper

1 teaspoon granulated garlic

1 teaspoon onion powder

1/2 teaspoon orange zest

1/2 cup tamari sauce

2 tablespoons peanut oil

1 lime, cut into wedges

Directions

- Sprinkle cod fillets with seasoned salt, pepper, garlic, and onion powder.
- In a mixing bowl, thoroughly combine orange zest, tamari sauce, and peanut oil. Place the fish in this sauce.
- Allow it to marinate for 2 hours in the refrigerator.
- Preheat your Air Fryer to 380 degrees for 5 minutes. Cook fish fillets for 12 minutes. Serve with lime wedges. Bon appétit!

51. Old Bay Calamari with Hot Mayo Sauce
(Ready in about 20 minutes | Servings 4)

This fantastic recipe is one of the best ways to cook the squid rings, also known as calamari. Squid is an excellent source of many essential nutrients such as vitamin B-12, copper, selenium, and so on.

Per serving: 405 Calories; 28.2g Fat; 9.7g Carbs; 28g Protein; 0.9g Sugars

Ingredients

1 pound squid, cleaned and cut into
   rings and tentacle pieces
3/4 cup almond flour
2 eggs
1 tablespoon Old Bay seasoning
Sea salt and ground black pepper, to
   taste
1 teaspoon shallot powder
1/2 cup parmesan cheese, grated
Coconut oil, place in an oil mister

For the sauce:
1/2 cup mayonnaise
2 tablespoons sour cream
1 teaspoon Sriracha

Directions

- Preheat your Air Fryer to 390 degrees F.
- Rinse the squid and pat it dry. Place the flour in a shallow bowl.
- In another bowl, whisk the eggs with Old Bay seasoning, salt, black pepper, and shallot powder.
- Add the parmesan cheese to the third shallow bowl.
- Dredge the squid pieces in the flour. Then, dip them into the egg mixture; afterwards, cover with the parmesan cheese.
- Arrange squids in the cooking basket. Spritz them with coconut oil and cook for 8 to 12 minutes, depending on the desired level of doneness. Work in batches.
- Then, make the sauce by whisking all of the sauce ingredients. Serve with warm fried squid and enjoy!

52. Bay Scallops with Ketchup Mayonnaise Sauce

(Ready in about 15 minutes | Servings 4)

What are you up to this evening? These richly seasoned scallops dipped in a creamy sauce will delight your taste buds.

Per serving: 291 Calories; 23.4g Fat; 4.9g Carbs; 14g Protein; 0.8g Sugars

Ingredients

For the Scallops:

1 pound bay scallops

1 ½ tablespoons extra-virgin olive oil

1 teaspoon cayenne pepper

1 teaspoon shallot powder

1/2 teaspoon ground bay leaf

1 teaspoon granulated garlic

Sea salt and ground black pepper, to
   taste

1/2 teaspoon dried rosemary

1 teaspoon dried basil

1/2 teaspoon chipotle powder

For the Dipping Sauce:

1/2 cup mayonnaise

1/4 cup tomato ketchup

1 tablespoon Worcestershire sauce

1/4 teaspoon ground black pepper

Directions

- Wash scallops and pat them dry. Transfer them to a re-sealable zipper storage bag.
- Add the remaining ingredients for the scallops and shake until scallops are covered with seasonings on all sides.
- Preheat your Air Fryer to 400 degrees F. Cook for 7 minutes, shaking halfway through cooking time.
- In the meantime, make the sauce by mixing the mayonnaise, ketchup, Worcestershire sauce, and ground black pepper. Serve with the prepared scallops and enjoy!

53. Tuna Steak in Beer Sauce
(Ready in about 20 minutes | Servings 4)

You must try this 5-star fish steak recipe! A beer marinade will add caramel-like flavor to your fish and reduce the cooking time in the Air Fryer. In this recipe, use light beers like pilsner or light lagers.

Per serving: 278 Calories; 12.5g Fat; 8.9g Carbs; 26.7g Protein; 1.7g Sugars

Ingredients

4 tuna steaks

Sea salt and ground black pepper, to
   taste

1 teaspoon cayenne pepper

1 cup beer

1/4 cup Worcestershire sauce

2 tablespoons safflower oil

2 tablespoons arrowroot powder

3 tablespoons water

Directions

- Place tuna steaks in a mixing bowl. Add the other ingredients and let it marinate for 1 hour in your refrigerator.
- Preheat your Air Fryer to 390 degrees F. Cook for 10 minutes or until tuna flakes easily with a fork.
- In the meantime, preheat a medium-sized saucepan over a moderate flame. Cook the marinade until it is reduced by half.
- Pour the sauce over prepared tuna steaks and serve immediately. Bon appétit!

54. Crab Tacos with Mexican Hot Sauce

(Ready in about 15 minutes | Servings 4)

Seafood is an extremely important part of every healthy diet. Crab is an excellent source of omega-3 fatty acids, vitamin B, and essential minerals.

Per serving: 605 Calories; 52.5g Fat; 7.9g Carbs; 24.6g Protein; 5g Sugars

Ingredients

1 cup Cheddar cheese, shredded
1/2 cup milk
1 egg, beaten
1 cup almond flour
Salt and ground black pepper, to taste
12 softshell crabs, cleaned

For the Sauce:
1 teaspoon Mexican hot sauce
1/2 cup mayonnaise
1 tablespoon pickles, chopped
2 tablespoons scallions, chopped
1 garlic clove, minced

Directions

- Start by preheating your oven to 350 degrees F.
- On a baking sheet lined with parchment paper place 1/4 cup piles of cheese. Press them down to make a tortilla shape.
- Bake for 5 to 7 minutes or until the edges of the cheese are delicately browned. Let the cheese tortillas cool for 2 to 3 minutes.
- Then, preheat your Air Fryer to 390 degrees F for 5 to 10 minutes.
- In a bowl, mix the milk, egg, flour, salt, and ground black pepper. Dip softshell crabs in the batter and transfer them to the cooking basket.
- Cook for 6 minutes or until they are thoroughly cooked.
- Then, in a mixing bowl, thoroughly combine Asian hot sauce, mayonnaise, pickles, scallions, and minced garlic.
- Assemble your tacos with crab, sauce, and tortillas. Bon appétit!

55. Cajun Fish Burger Bowls

(Ready in about 15 minutes | Servings 4)

Make these amazing fish burgers and bring summer into your kitchen! This time we used sole, but cod, halibut, and salmon work well too.

Per serving: 221 Calories; 12.9g Fat; 3.8g Carbs; 21.3g Protein; 1.1g Sugars

Ingredients

1 pound sole fish, chopped

1 teaspoon Cajun spice mix

1 shallot, finely chopped

1 garlic clove, minced

1 egg

2 tablespoons buttermilk

1/2 cup parmesan cheese, grated

1 handful mixed lettuce

4 tablespoons mayonnaise

Directions

- Add sole fish, Cajun spice mix, shallot, garlic, egg and buttermilk to your food processor; process until everything is well combined.
- Place the cheese in a shallow dish.
- Shape the mixture into 4 patties; coat each patty with cheese. Cook fish burgers in the preheated Air Fryer at 390 degrees F for 8 minutes.
- Afterwards, assemble the bowls with mixed lettuce, fish patties and mayonnaise. Bon appétit!

56. Grilled and Ginger-Glazed Halibut Steak
(Ready in about 25 minutes | Servings 2)

With its velvety texture, halibut is the perfect fish for this amazing dish, but Arctic char or black cod can be used as well. A sweet, spicy and jellied glaze balances a rich flavor of halibut. Perfect!

Per serving: 529 Calories; 43.8g Fat; 8.9g Carbs; 24.9g Protein; 5.6g Sugars

Ingredients

1/2 cup ketchup

3 tablespoons olive oil

1 tablespoon lemon juice

1/2 teaspoon fresh ginger, grated

2 tablespoons Erythritol

1 teaspoon onion powder

1 teaspoon dried parsley flakes

1 teaspoon garlic, minced

Salt and freshly ground black pepper, to taste

2 (2-inch thick) halibut steaks

Directions

- Place all of the above ingredients in a mixing dish; wrap with foil and transfer to your refrigerator. Allow it to marinate for 1 hour.
- In the meantime, preheat your Air Fryer to 400 degrees F. Remove the halibut steaks from the marinade and cook them for 10 minutes or until they are opaque throughout.
- Next, preheat a medium-sized saucepan over a moderate flame. Cook the marinade until it is reduced by half.
- Pour the glaze over the fish. Place under a broiler for 5 minutes or until the halibut steaks are browned. Eat warm. Bon appétit!

VEGETABLES & SIDE DISHES

57. Hot and Spicy Broccoli with Peppers

(Ready in about 20 minutes | Servings 4)

Looking for a surprisingly sensational and refreshing side dish? Try this easy and delicious vegetable dish tonight!

Per serving: 95 Calories; 6.2g Fat; 8.7g Carbs; 3.5g Protein; 2,2g Sugars

Ingredients

1 pound broccoli, broken into florets

1 bell pepper, chopped

1 serrano pepper, chopped

2 tablespoons butter, melted

2 spring onions, chopped

2 cloves garlic, minced

1 tablespoon coconut aminos

Sea salt and ground black pepper, to taste

1/2 teaspoon cayenne pepper

1/2 teaspoon chipotle powder

Directions

- Preheat your Air Fryer to 400 degrees F.
- Brush broccoli and peppers with melted butter and transfer to a cooking basket.
- Add peppers to the preheated Air Fryer and cook for 9 minutes, shaking once or twice. Add the remaining ingredients, along with broccoli.
- Cook an additional 6 minutes. Serve immediately and enjoy!

58. Bok Choy Salad with Montrachet

(Ready in about 50 minutes + chilling time | Servings 4)

You can't go wrong with a combo of richly seasoned veggies and mild, creamy goat cheese. Serve with grilled fish.

Per serving: 207 Calories; 16.2g Fat; 5g Carbs; 10.9g Protein; 3g Sugars

Ingredients

1 pound Bok choy

1/4 cup extra-virgin olive oil

2 teaspoons Dijon mustard

2 tablespoons balsamic vinegar

Coarse salt and freshly ground black

pepper, to taste

2 cups baby arugula

2 cloves garlic, minced

4 ounces Montrachet cheese, crumbled

Directions

- Preheat your Air Fryer to 390 degrees F.
- Cook your Bok choy for 10 minutes, turning halfway through the cooking time. Cut Bok choy into thin slices using a sharp kitchen knife; transfer to a salad bowl.
- In a small mixing dish, thoroughly combine olive oil, mustard, balsamic vinegar, salt, and black pepper.
- Toss Bok choy with arugula, garlic, and the prepared vinaigrette. Top with crumbled Montrachet cheese and serve well-chilled. Bon appétit!

59. Roasted Vegetables with Sriracha Mayo

(Ready in about 20 minutes | Servings 4)

Roasted vegetables are always a good idea for any family gathering. You just have to find your favorite combo.

Per serving: 253 Calories; 23.6g Fat; 9.5g Carbs; 3.5g Protein; 5.5g Sugars

Ingredients

2 Roma tomatoes, halved

1/2 pound eggplant, cubed

1/2 pound mushrooms, quartered

1 red onion, sliced

1 teaspoon garlic, minced

1/4 cup butter, melted

1 teaspoon cayenne pepper

1/2 teaspoon dried dill

1/2 teaspoon dried basil

1/2 teaspoon dried rosemary

Salt and ground black pepper, to taste

1/2 cup mayonnaise

1/2 teaspoon Sriracha

Directions

- Preheat your Air Fryer to 380 degrees F.
- Spritz the inside of a baking pan with a nonstick cooking spray. Add the vegetables together with butter and seasonings to the baking pan.
- Place the pan in the Air Fryer and roast the vegetables for 10 minutes.
- Increase the temperature to 400 degrees F. Cook an additional 5 minutes.
- In the meantime, mix the mayonnaise with Sriracha. Serve with warm vegetables. Bon appétit!

60. Beef and Mushroom Stuffed Zucchini
(Ready in about 35 minutes | Servings 4)

Here's a classic recipe for an old-fashioned stuffed zucchini! Serve with a fresh salad and enjoy!

Per serving: 215 Calories; 13.6g Fat; 9.6g Carbs; 16.6g Protein; 3.5g Sugars

Ingredients

1 pound zucchini, cut in half lengthwise
1 tablespoon olive oil
1 yellow onion, chopped
1/2 pound ground beef
1/2 pound button mushrooms,
   chopped

1 Serrano pepper, chopped
1 teaspoon garlic paste
Salt and ground black pepper, to taste
1 tomato, pureed
1/2 tablespoon soy sauce
1 sprig dried rosemary, leaves picked

Directions

- Scoop out the pulp of zucchini with a teaspoon, leaving 1/2-inch shells. Finely chop the pulp.
- Preheat the oil in a sauté pan over a moderate heat. Now, sweat the onion for 2 to 3 minutes.
- Add the ground beef, mushrooms, Serrano pepper and garlic paste; continue to cook an additional 4 minutes. Sprinkle with salt and pepper; cover and set it aside.
- Add the pureed tomato, soy sauce, and dried rosemary. Add the zucchini pulp and mix to combine.
- Divide the mixture among zucchini boats and transfer them to a lightly greased baking pan.
- Next, preheat your Air Fryer to 400 degrees F. Place the baking pan in your Air Fryer and bake for 17 minutes. Serve warm. Bon appétit!

61. Easy Cauliflower Au Gratin

(Ready in about 40 minutes | Servings 6)

This top-rated vegetarian recipe is so easy to prepare in the Air Fryer. We used Cheddar cheese but feel free to use a combination of Gruyere and Parmesan instead.

Per serving: 247 Calories; 17.5g Fat; 9.5g Carbs; 14.7g Protein; 5.2g Sugars

Ingredients

1 ½ pounds cauliflower, cut into florets
1/2 cup onion, chopped
1 tablespoon butter, softened
1 cup milk

2 cups Cheddar cheese, shredded
Kosher salt and ground black pepper,
   to taste

Directions

- Place a steamer insert into a pan and fill with water. Bring water to a boil. Then, steam cauliflower for 6 minutes.
- Then, preheat the Air Fryer to 400 degrees F.
- Arrange the cauliflower in a lightly greased baking pan. Top with chopped onion.
- In a mixing dish, thoroughly combine the butter, milk, cheese, salt and black pepper. Pour the mixture over the cauliflower in the baking pan. Cook for 20 minutes in your Air Fryer.
- Scatter the cheese over the top and cook an additional 12 minutes or until cheese is melted. Enjoy!

62. Cheesy Veggie Fried Balls
(Ready in about 30 minutes | Servings 5)

It doesn't have to be hard to get your children to eat vegetables! These balls are fun to eat and easy to make in the Air Fryer.

Per serving: 281 Calories; 21.7g Fat; 4.1g Carbs; 17.8g Protein; 1.4g Sugars

Ingredients

2 cups zucchini, grated
1 cup cauliflower, riced
1 cup Romano cheese, freshly grated
1 ½ cups Colby cheese, freshly grated
1/2 teaspoon dried dill weed

1 teaspoon garlic powder
1 teaspoon paprika
Salt and pepper, to taste
1 egg, beaten

Directions

- Mix all of the above ingredients until everything is well incorporated.
- Take 1 tablespoon of the veggie mixture and roll into a ball. Transfer it to the preheated Air Fryer.
- Repeat until you run out of ingredients. Cook at 360 degrees F for 15 minutes or until thoroughly cooked and crispy.
- Work in batches and transfer to a nice serving platter. Bon appétit!

63. Crispy Zucchini with Ranch Dressing
(Ready in about 30 minutes | Servings 5)

What are you up to tonight? A grab-and-go quick snack or an elegant party dinner? These cheesy zucchini bites are both, simple and sophisticated.

Per serving: 435 Calories; 37.1g Fat; 9.6g Carbs; 17.9g Protein; 3g Sugars

Ingredients

2 eggs

1/4 cup buttermilk

1 teaspoon dried thyme

1/2 teaspoon dried oregano

1/2 teaspoon dried basil

1/2 teaspoon garlic powder

1 cup Romano cheese, grated

1 cup Asiago cheese, freshly grated

1 pound zucchini, peeled and quartered lengthwise

1 cup ranch dressing

Directions

- Preheat your Air Fryer to 400 degrees F.
- In a shallow dish, whisk the eggs with buttermilk until frothy.
- Then, place thyme, oregano, basil, garlic powder, Romano and Asiago cheese in a separate bowl.
- Dip each piece of zucchini in the egg/buttermilk mixture; then, roll them into the cheese/chips mixture.
- Arrange zucchinis in a cooking basket and brush them with olive oil. Cook for 12 minutes, shaking halfway through the cooking time.
- Work in batches and transfer to a serving platter. Serve with ranch dressing. Enjoy!

64. Jicama Fries with Greek Dipping Sauce

(Ready in about 30 minutes | Servings 4)

If you are looking for guilt-free vegetable fries, dig into this wonderful snack with a yogurt dip. The Air Fryer is the perfect kitchen tool for this recipe.

Per serving: 111 Calories; 7.8g Fat; 9g Carbs; 1.6g Protein; 2.9g Sugars

Ingredients

1 pound jicama, trimmed and slice into sticks

1 teaspoon coarse salt

1/4 teaspoon grated nutmeg

2 tablespoons olive oil

The Sauce:

1/2 cup full-fat Greek yogurt

1 teaspoon lemon juice

1/2 teaspoon sea salt

1 teaspoon garlic, minced

1/2 teaspoon black pepper, freshly cracked

Directions

- Place jicama sticks in the cooking basket in a single layer. Sprinkle with salt and nutmeg. Drizzle with olive oil.
- Cook in the preheated Air Fryer at 400 degrees F for 4 to 5 minutes. Work in batches and give them a shake twice during cooking.
- Meanwhile, make Greek dipping sauce by mixing yogurt, lemon juice, sea salt, garlic and pepper.
- Serve with roasted carrots and enjoy!

65. Classic Roasted Brussels Sprouts

(Ready in about 20 minutes | Servings 4)

These roasted Brussels sprouts will be gone in no time so make sure to double the recipe. Brussels sprouts have many health benefits. They improve bone health, manage diabetes and help you to achieve your ideal body weight.

Per serving: 96 Calories; 7g Fat; 7.6g Carbs; 2.9g Protein; 1.8g Sugars

Ingredients

3/4 pound Brussels sprouts

2 tablespoons olive oil

1 teaspoon coarse salt

1/2 teaspoon ground black pepper

1/2 teaspoon smoked paprika

Directions

- Preheat your Air Fryer to 380 degrees F.
- Toss Brussels sprouts with olive oil, salt, black pepper, and paprika.
- Cook for 15 minutes or until they are crisp-tender, shaking twice during cooking.
- Serve warm with your favorite dipping sauce. Bon appétit!

66. Cauliflower and Onion Pakoras
(Ready in about 20 minutes | Servings 4)

Here's a completely new way to eat your cauliflower. Kids will love these perfectly spiced, crunchy bites.

Per serving: 184 Calories; 15.4g Fat; 8.6g Carbs; 5.9g Protein; 2.4g Sugars

Ingredients

1 ½ cups cauliflower, chopped

1/2 onion, finely chopped

1 garlic clove, minced

1 teaspoon fresh ginger, grated

Salt and ground black pepper, to taste

1 teaspoon paprika

1 teaspoon curry powder

1/2 teaspoon garam masala

1 cup almond flour

1/2 teaspoon baking powder

1 tablespoon olive oil

Water, as needed

Directions

- Add the cauliflower, onion, garlic and ginger to a mixing bowl. Now, sprinkle, with salt, pepper, paprika, curry powder, and garam masala; stir to combine well.
- Now, stir in the flour and baking powder; mix again.
- Add olive oil; then, pour in water until soft dough forms. The mixture should not be too thick. Actually, you would be able to form the mixture into patties.
- Preheat your Air Fryer to 380 degrees F. Place the prepared patties in your Air Fryer and cook for 15 minutes, turning halfway through cooking time. Bon appétit!

67. Korokke with Cheddar cheese
(Ready in about 1 hour | Servings 5)

Korokke is traditional Japanese croquettes that are made of potatoes and cheese. You can use kohlrabi in this recipe to make it keto friendly. You can also add seafood, cooked chopped meat or vegetables.

Per serving: 378 Calories; 28.1g Fat; 9.8g Carbs; 22.7g Protein; 2.3g Sugars

Ingredients

3/4 pound kohlrabi stems and roots removed

2 eggs, whisked

8 ounces Cheddar cheese, preferably freshly grated

1/2 cup almond flour

1/2 teaspoon seasoned salt

1/3 teaspoon ground black pepper

4 ounces Parmesan cheese, grated

Tonkatsu sauce, to serve

Directions

- Place kohlrabi in a pan of boiling water; simmer for 20 to 25 minutes.
- Mash the kohlrabi and allow them to cool completely. Stir in the eggs, Cheddar cheese, almond flour, salt, and black pepper.
- Shape the mixture into 4 cakes and cover with grated parmesan cheese.
- Preheat your Air Fryer to 390 degrees F. Cook for 10 minutes or until brown on the outside. Serve with Tonkatsu sauce if desired. Enjoy!

68. Parmesan Green Beans with Wasabi Sauce
(Ready in about 20 minutes | Servings 4)

Have you ever had green beans from an Air Fryer? It's time to try something new! A crisp-tender green beans with a pungent wasabi sauce is your next favorite snack under 200 calories.

Per serving: 149 Calories; 10.4g Fat; 9.2g Carbs; 5.9g Protein; 0.9g Sugars

Ingredients

1 pound green beans
1 tablespoon sesame oil
1/2 cup parmesan cheese, grated
1 teaspoon paprika
Seasoned salt to taste ground black
    pepper, to taste

For the Sauce:
1/2 cup sour cream
1 teaspoon wasabi paste
Salt, to taste

Directions

- Bring a lightly salted water to a boil; boil the green beans for 2 minutes. Now, drain green beans and dry them on a kitchen towel. Drizzle with sesame oil.
- In a mixing bowl, thoroughly combine parmesan cheese, paprika, salt, and black pepper. Dip green beans in this mixture, coating all sides.
- Cook green beans in your Air Fryer at 390 degrees F for 10 minutes.
- Then, whisk the sour cream with wasabi paste and salt to make the sauce. Serve with fried green beans and enjoy!

69. Mediterranean-Style Vegetable Rounds
(Ready in about 30 minutes | Servings 4)

This side dish is both, light and fulfilling. Air-fried vegetable rounds are seasoned with the perfect blend of good-quality Mediterranean aromatics. Serve with white fish fillets.
Per serving: 96 Calories; 6.1g Fat; 8.2g Carbs; 1.4g Protein; 4.9g Sugars

Ingredients

1 (1 1/4-pound) eggplant, slice into
   1-inch thick rounds
1 red onion, sliced
2 tablespoons butter, melted
Sea salt and ground black pepper, to
   taste

1/2 teaspoon dried oregano
1/2 teaspoon garlic powder
1/2 teaspoon dried basil
1/2 teaspoon dried rosemary
1/4 teaspoon dried thyme

Directions

- Preheat your Air Fryer to 380 degrees F.
- Brush eggplants and onion with melted butter. Now, toss them with seasoning until they are well covered.
- Arrange the slices of eggplant in the cooking basket; cook for 20 minutes, flipping half-way through cooking time.
- Now, add the slices of onion and cook an additional 10 minutes. Serve immediately and enjoy!

70. Broccoli Stuffed Mushrooms with Cheese
(Ready in about 15 minutes | Servings 4)

As you probably already know, mushrooms possess a remarkable nutritional composition. For this recipe, choose the mushrooms of similar size to ensure even cooking.
Per serving: 131 Calories; 9.1g Fat; 4.5g Carbs; 9.1g Protein; 1.8g Sugars

Ingredients

8 large white button mushrooms, cleaned and stems removed
1 cup broccoli, chopped
1 cup Pepper-Jack cheese grated
2 tablespoons scallions, minced
2 garlic cloves, minced

1 teaspoon paprika
Salt and ground black pepper, to your liking
1/4 cup fresh Italian parsley leaves, chopped

Directions

- Give the mushrooms a quick shower and pat them dry as best as you can.
- In a mixing bowl, thoroughly combine broccoli with cheese, scallions, garlic, paprika, salt and black pepper.
- Then, divide the mixture among mushroom caps.
- Preheat your Air Fryer to 390 degrees F. Cook your mushrooms for 8 minutes or until they are thoroughly cooked.
- Transfer the mushrooms to a serving platter, garnish with Italian parsley and serve.

FAST SNACKS & APPETIZERS

71. Garlic and Oregano Bites
(Ready in about 10 minutes | Servings 2)

These crispy, garlicky bites are simply irresistible. Cauliflower is rich in fiber, vitamins, and minerals such as magnesium and phosphorus.

Per serving: 166 Calories; 14.4g Fat; 8.4g Carbs; 3.2g Protein; 3.2g Sugars

Ingredients

3/4 pound cauliflower, broken into florets

2 tablespoons extra-virgin olive oil

1/4 teaspoon sea salt

1/2 teaspoon oregano

1 teaspoon granulated garlic

Directions

- Toss cauliflower with olive oil, salt, oregano, and garlic.
- Preheat the Air Fryer to 400 degrees F. Cook for 9 minutes or until golden brown, shaking halfway through cooking time.
- Serve and enjoy!

72. Baked Avocado Chips
(Ready in about 25 minutes | Servings 2)

If you like to experiment with your food, try adding a pinch of ground nutmeg to this chips; it will make a huge difference in the flavor.

Per serving: 129 Calories; 9.4g Fat; 4.1g Carbs; 7.1g Protein; 0.2g Sugars

Ingredients

1 large ripe avocado, mashed
1 tablespoon freshly squeezed lemon
   juice
1 teaspoon avocado oil
1/4 teaspoon ground cloves

1/2 cup Parmesan cheese, freshly grated
1/2 teaspoon garlic powder
1/2 teaspoon Italian seasoning
Kosher salt and ground black pepper,
   to taste

Directions

- Mix all of the above ingredients.
- Divide the mixture into balls; flatten each ball with a fork and transfer them to a foil-lined baking pan.
- Put the baking pan into the Air Fryer and bake your chips
- Preheat your Air Fryer to 320 degrees F. Bake for 15 minutes, flipping them over around halfway through cooking time. Bon appétit!

73. Swiss Chard Chips with Avocado Dip
(Ready in about 15 minutes | Servings 6)

Thanks to the Air Fryer, you can enjoy super-healthy snacks without any guilt. This is a great idea for a dinner party; just make sure to make a double batch.

Per serving: 135 Calories; 11.6g Fat; 7.2g Carbs; 2.7g Protein; 1.1g Sugars

Ingredients

1 pound Swiss chard, ribs cut out

2 tablespoons sesame oil

Salt and ground black pepper, to taste

1 teaspoon garlic powder

1 teaspoon cayenne pepper

For the Dipping Sauce:

1 avocado, peeled an pitted

1/2 cup sour cream

2 tablespoons fresh chives, chopped

1 tablespoon fresh lemon juice

1 teaspoon chili pepper, deveined and minced

Sea salt, to taste

Directions

- Toss Swiss chard with sesame oil, salt, black pepper, garlic powder, and cayenne pepper.
- Preheat your Air Fryer to 380 degrees F. Cook for 4 minutes or until crisp, shaking halfway through cooking time.
- In the meantime, blitz avocado, sour cream, chives, lemon juice, chili pepper, and salt in your food processor.
- Process until everything is well blended. Serve with Swiss chard chips and enjoy!

74. Famous Buffalo-Style Wings
(Ready in about 45 minutes | Servings 6)

Here's a classic recipe for chicken wings that you shouldn't miss! It is delicious, fun to eat, and easy to prepare. Serve on any occasion and make a great impression!
Per serving: 295 Calories; 20.5g Fat; 3g Carbs; 25.3g Protein; 1.6g Sugars

Ingredients

1 cup almond flour
Sea salt and ground black pepper, to
    taste
1 teaspoon garlic powder
1/2 teaspoon onion powder
1 teaspoon paprika

1 ¼ pounds chicken wings, split at the
    joint
1/4 cup hot sauce, or to taste
1 teaspoon Worcestershire sauce
1/2 cup Maytag cheese, crumbled

Directions

- Preheat your Air Fryer to 380 degrees F.
- In a mixing dish, combine the flour, salt, black pepper, garlic powder, onion powder, and paprika. Now, dredge the wings in the seasoned flour mixture and coat on all sides.
- Transfer the wings to a cooking basket and spritz them with a nonstick cooking spray.
- Cook for 22 minutes in the Preheated Air Fryer or until cooked through. Work in batches until you run out of ingredients.
- Toss the fried chicken wings with hot sauce and Worcestershire sauce. Scatter crumbled cheese over warm wings and serve immediately. Bon appétit!

75. Zucchini Chips with Chili Mayo
(Ready in about 25 minutes | Servings 6)

An Air Fryer isn't just for making potato chips. You can use almost every veggie to make chips, including zucchini, kale, carrots, parsnips, and so on.

Per serving: 145 Calories; 11.5g Fat; 5.1g Carbs; 6.5g Protein; 2g Sugars

Ingredients

2 eggs

2 tablespoons water

1/2 cup Romano cheese, grated

1 ½ tablespoons olive oil

2 zucchinis, peeled and thinly sliced

Sea salt ground black pepper, to taste

1/2 teaspoon cayenne pepper

1/4 cup mayonnaise

1 teaspoon chili sauce

Directions

- Whisk the eggs with water in a shallow dish. Mix Romano cheese and olive oil in a separate shallow dish.
- Dip the zucchini slices first in the egg wash; then, dredge into cheese mixture. Sprinkle with the salt, black pepper, and cayenne.
- Preheat your Air Fryer to 370 degrees F. Cook for 15 minutes, shaking halfway through cooking time.
- In a mixing dish, whisk the mayonnaise with chili sauce. Serve with zucchini sticks. Bon appétit!

76. Cheese-Stuffed Cocktail Meatballs
(Ready in about 15 minutes | Servings 6)

Here's a new twist on an old favorite! Kids of all ages will love these flavorful balls!
Per serving: 312 Calories; 20.2g Fat; 7.9g Carbs; 25.3g Protein; 1g Sugars

Ingredients

1/2 pound ground beef
1/2 pound sausage, crumbled
1 ¼ cups dried bread flakes
1 garlic clove, minced
Sea salt and ground black pepper, to

taste
1/2 teaspoon hot paprika
1/4 teaspoon ground bay leaf
2 eggs
4 ounces Monterey Jack cheese, cubed

Directions

- Preheat your Air Fryer to 380 degrees F.
- In a mixing bowl, thoroughly combine ground beef, sausage, dried bread flakes, garlic, salt, pepper, paprika, ground bay leaf, and eggs.
- Shape the mixture into meatballs. Add 1 cheese cube to the center of each ball, sealing it inside.
- Spritz meatballs with a nonstick cooking spray. Cook for 10 minutes, shaking once or twice during cooking. Serve with cocktail sticks and enjoy!

77. Cocktail Lil Smokies
(Ready in about 25 minutes | Servings 8)

Lil smokies are always a good idea, right? They are much better with a quick, delicate sauce. The brown sugar will bring the perfect amount of sweetness to the sauce. Enjoy!

Per serving: 332 Calories; 28.3g Fat; 5.4g Carbs; 12.2g Protein; 4.2g Sugars

Ingredients

1 (28-ounce) package mini smoked
    sausage links

1/2 cup ketchup

1/4 cup dry white wine

1/4 cup water

1 tablespoons stone ground mustard

Directions

- Start by preheating your Air Fryer to 380 degrees F.
- Prick the sausages and transfer them to a baking pan. Cook in the preheated Air Fryer for 15 minutes, turning halfway through cooking time.
- Work in two batches to make sure that sausages don't touch with each other.
- In the meantime, preheat a saucepan over a moderately high flame. Cook ketchup, wine, water, and mustard until it is thickened.
- Heat off; add the prepared sausages to the saucepan and stir to combine. Serve with toothpicks. Bon appétit!

78. Father's Day Crispy Pork Crackling
(Ready in about 25 minutes | Servings 8)

Don't be fooled by the simplicity of pork skin, it makes an excellent, cheat-worthy snack. From start to finish, this extraordinary snack only takes 25 minutes to make.
Per serving: 268 Calories; 26.7g Fat; 3.4g Carbs; 3.6g Protein; 1.6g Sugars

Ingredients

2 sheets of pork skin

1 tablespoon salt

1/2 teaspoon cayenne pepper

1 teaspoon garlic powder

3 tablespoons soy sauce

3 tablespoons fresh lemon juice

1 chili pepper, chopped

2 garlic cloves

1 tablespoon tahini

Directions

- Wash pork skins and prick them (you can use a salami pricker).
- Rub with the salt, cayenne pepper, and garlic powder; place in your refrigerator overnight.
- Preheat your Air Fryer to 400 degrees F. Cook pork skin on a grill pan for 12 minutes; repeat with the other pork skin.
- Remove from the Air Fryer; cut into strips using kitchen tongs and scissors.
- In the meantime, make the dipping sauce by mixing the remaining ingredients in a food processor. Serve pork cracklings with the sauce on the side. Enjoy!

79. Herbed Tomato Chips with Garlic Mayo

(Ready in about 20 minutes | Servings 4)

If you're looking to add more antioxidants to your diet, this recipe is a great go-to. Yes, tomato chips! It is an unexpected, chip, and healthy snack.

Per serving: 144 Calories; 15g Fat; 2.1g Carbs; 0.5g Protein; 1g Sugars

Ingredients

3 tomatoes, thinly sliced

3 teaspoons olive oil

Sea salt and ground black pepper, to taste

1 teaspoon dried rosemary, chopped

1 teaspoon dried sage, crushed

1/2 cup full-fat mayonnaise

2 garlic cloves, smashed

1 teaspoon cayenne pepper

Directions

- Begin by preheating your Air Fryer to 360 degrees F. Toss the tomato slices with olive oil, salt, black pepper, rosemary, and sage.
- Cook for 10 minutes, flipping halfway through cooking time. Meanwhile, mix the mayonnaise, garlic, and cayenne pepper in a bowl.
- Serve tomato chips with the garlic mayo or store in an airtight container. Bon appétit!

80. Bacon-Wrapped Mushrooms

(Ready in about 20 minutes | Servings 4)

You can add your favorite combo of seasonings and cheese, so get creative! This recipe can be doubled or tripled easily.

Per serving: 365 Calories; 30.9g Fat; 9.1g Carbs; 12.3g Protein; 5.3g Sugars

Ingredients

12 medium fresh mushrooms
12 strips of bacon

1/2 cup barbecue sauce

Directions

- Start by preheating your Air Fryer to 395 degrees F.
- Wrap each mushroom with a strip of bacon; secure with a toothpick. Arrange bacon-wrapped mushrooms in a cooking basket. Add barbecue sauce.
- Cook bacon-wrapped mushrooms for 10 minutes, flipping them halfway through cooking time.
- Transfer to a serving platter and enjoy!

81. Easy Celery Chips
(Ready in about 20 minutes | Servings 4)

Try a healthy twist on a favorite salty snack. Thinly slice your veggies into chips with a mandolin. Then, cook them in the Air Fryer. Simple like that.

Per serving: 140 Calories; 11.8g Fat; 7.4g Carbs; 1.8g Protein; 3.1g Sugars

Ingredients

1/4 cup butter, melted
1 teaspoon garlic paste
2 tablespoons coconut amino

Salt and pepper, to taste
2 ½ tablespoons arrowroot powder
1 ½ pounds celery, sliced

Directions

- Mix the butter, garlic paste, coconut amino, salt, pepper, and arrowroot in a large bowl. Mix well to form a smooth paste; add a tablespoon of water or two, as needed.
- Add the celery slices to the bowl; mix well until they're coated.
- Now, preheat your Air Fryer to 380 degrees F.
- Cook your veggie chips for 15 minutes, flipping them halfway through cooking time. Consume within 3 days. Bon appétit!

82. The Best Onion Rings Ever
(Ready in about 15 minutes | Servings 6)

Make this ultimate comfort, "good-for-you" snack and delight your guests for the next cocktail party!

Per serving: 153 Calories; 11.7g Fat; 5g Carbs; 6.9g Protein; 2.1g Sugars

Ingredients

1/2 cup Parmesan cheese, grated
1/2 cup pork rinds, crushed
Salt and ground black pepper, to taste
1/2 teaspoon paprika

2 egg whites
2 yellow onions, sliced into rings
2 tablespoons canola oil

Directions

- Begin by preheating your Air Fryer to 400 degrees F for 5 minutes.
- Mix Parmesan cheese, pork rinds, salt, pepper, and paprika. In another bowl, whisk the egg whites.
- Dip onion rings into egg whites; then, coat them with parmesan mixture on all sides. Brush with canola oil and transfer to the Air Fryer cooking basket.
- Cook for 7 minutes, shaking several times during the cooking process; work in batches and serve with your favorite sauce for dipping. Bon appétit!

83. Mozzarella Cheese Sticks

(Ready in about 15 minutes | Servings 4)

This is a great and easy way to control cravings for unhealthy foods. You can make a double batch and keep these sticks in your freezer for a quick snack on any occasion!

Per serving: 145 Calories; 9g Fat; 15.1g Carbs; 3.4g Protein; 3.2g Sugars

Ingredients

1/4 cup almond flour

1/4 cup Parmesan cheese the powdered kind in a can

1 tablespoon coconut flour

1 teaspoon onion powder

1 teaspoon garlic powder

1/2 teaspoon salt

1/2 teaspoon chili flakes

1 egg, beaten

1 (10-ounce) package part skim mozzarella string cheese

Directions

- Start by preheating the Air Fryer to 370 degrees F.
- Place almond flour, Parmesan cheese, coconut flour, onion powder, garlic powder, salt and chili flakes in a zipper sandwich bag. Shake bag to blend.
- Add beaten egg. Dip each cheese stick in this mixture. Cook for 5 minutes in the preheated Air Fryer.
- Serve immediately. Bon appétit!

EGGS & DAIRY

84. Classic Deviled Eggs

(Ready in about 20 minutes + chilling time | Servings 3)

With delicious and elegant deviled eggs, everything is looking and tasting good. Double the recipe and enjoy your dinner party.

Per serving: 191 Calories; 14.7g Fat; 1.3g Carbs; 12.3g Protein; 0.5g Sugars

Ingredients

6 medium-sized cold eggs
1/4 cup mayonnaise
1 teaspoon Dijon mustard
1 teaspoon rice vinegar

Sea salt and freshly ground black pepper, to taste
Spanish paprika, for garnish

Directions

- Place a wire rack inside the air fryer basket; lower the eggs onto the rack.
- Cook at 250 degrees F for 16 minutes.
- Remove hard-boiled eggs from the Air Fryer and transfer them to a bowl of cold water for 10 minutes. Peel the eggs.
- Slice the eggs in half lengthwise, removing yolks to a mixing bowl. Then, place the whites on a serving platter.
- Add mayo, mustard, rice vinegar, salt, and black pepper to the mixing bowl; mix until everything is well incorporated.
- Divide the mixture between egg whites. Sprinkle with Spanish paprika and serve well chilled. Bon appétit!

85. Mushroom and Scallion Omelet
(Ready in about 20 minutes | Servings 2)

Never underestimate the power of eggs and mushrooms – they are filling, healthy and easy to cook in an Air Fryer.

Per serving: 314 Calories; 20.6g Fat; 9.3g Carbs; 23.4g Protein; 6.2g Sugars

Ingredients

4 eggs

1/2 cup milk

1/2 teaspoon sea salt

1/4 teaspoon red pepper flakes, crushed

1 bell pepper, chopped

1/2 cup scallions, chopped

1 cup button mushrooms, chopped

1/2 cup Monterey-Jack cheese, shredded

Directions

- Start by preheating the Air Fryer to 360 degrees F.
- Thoroughly combine the eggs and milk using a wire whisk. Sprinkle with salt and red pepper flakes.
- Stir in vegetables and mix again. Pour the mixture into a baking pan. Place the pan in the air fryer basket.
- Cook approximately 5 minutes; scatter the shredded cheese over the top and cook for a further 4 minutes.
- Slice the omelet into two halves and serve. Bon appétit!

86. Elegant Scotch Eggs

(Ready in about 20 minutes | Servings 5)

Elegant and delicious scotch eggs go well with Iceberg lettuce, hot tomato sauce and pickled onions. Do not forget to add a hot sauce to spice it up!

Per serving: 411 Calories; 23.8g Fat; 7g Carbs; 40g Protein; 1.4g Sugars

Ingredients

1/2 cup scallion, finely chopped

2 cloves garlic, minced

Sea salt and ground black pepper, to taste

1 pound ground beef

1 teaspoon hot sauce

1/2 cup almond flour

1 raw egg

3 tablespoons milk

1 ½ cups Parmesan cheese, grated

5 eggs, hard-boiled

Directions

- Start by preheating your Air Fryer to 360 degrees F. Mix the scallions, garlic, salt, black pepper, ground beef, and hot sauce; mix until everything is well incorporated.
- Then, create a breading station. In a shallow bowl, place almond flour. In the second bowl, whisk the raw egg with milk. Finally, in the third bowl, place Parmesan cheese.
- Dip each cooked egg in the almond flour mixture. Divide meat mixture into five balls. Fold them around hard cooked eggs using your hands.
- Then, dip eggs into flour again; dip in egg/milk mixture. Finally, roll them in grated cheese to coat on all sides.
- Transfer scotch eggs to the Air Fryer basket and cook for 16 minutes. Enjoy!

87. Classic Scrambled Eggs
(Ready in about 15 minutes | Servings 5)

Learning how to make scrambled eggs in an Air Fryer can be fun! Take your eggs to a whole new level by adding cheese, salsa or veggies.

Per serving: 330 Calories; 30.1g Fat; 2g Carbs; 18g Protein; 1.3g Sugars

Ingredients

2 tablespoons butter

4 eggs

1/2 teaspoon sea salt

1/4 teaspoon ground black pepper

1/4 teaspoon red pepper flakes

1/2 teaspoon dried parsley flakes

Directions

- Start by preheating your Air Fryer to 280 degrees F. Once hot, melt the butter.
- In a mixing bowl, whisk the eggs with seasonings.
- Cook for 9 to 11 minutes until fluffy and no visible liquid egg remains. Serve warm.

88. Sunday Two-Cheese Balls

(Ready in about1 hour 15 minutes | Servings 5)

Seriously, these balls are weeknight dinner saviors. They are cheap, delicious and easy to make on busy weeknights!

Per serving: 341 Calories; 25.5g Fat; 6.7g Carbs; 21.3g Protein; 0.5g Sugars

Ingredients

- 1 ½ cups Colby cheese, preferably freshly grated
- 2 tablespoons almond flour
- 1 teaspoon granulated garlic
- Salt and ground black pepper, to taste
- 1/2 teaspoon chili flakes
- 2 eggs
- 1 ½ cups Parmesan, grated

Directions

- Mix Colby cheese, almond flour, granulated garlic, salt, and black pepper until everything is well incorporated.
- Shape the mixture into bite-size balls and transfer to your freezer for 1 hour.
- Whisk the eggs in a mixing bowl. In another bowl, place grated parmesan cheese.
- Dip the balls in the beaten eggs. Roll the balls over Parmesan cheese; arrange balls on a baking sheet that is lined with a parchment paper.
- Cook at 390 degrees F for 11 minutes; rotating frequently. Bon appétit!

89. Cauliflower Mozza Balls

(Ready in about 15 minutes | Servings 4)

Here is an insanely easy snack that is perfect for your birthday party! It is also dinner-worthy and kid-friendly.

Per serving: 255 Calories; 19.3g Fat; 9.4g Carbs; 13.4g Protein; 1.6g Sugars

Ingredients

1/2 head cauliflower

1/2 cup almond flour

3 ounces mozzarella cheese, shredded

2 eggs

1 teaspoon baking powder

1/2 teaspoon sea salt

1/4 teaspoon ground black pepper

6 tablespoons flaxseed meal

Directions

- Pulse your cauliflower in a food possessor until it is well processed.
- Add the flour, cheese, eggs, baking powder, salt, and black pepper; mix until everything is well incorporated.
- Shape this mixture into balls; coat the balls with flaxseed meal. Cook in the preheated Air Fryer at 390 degrees F for 12 minutes; rotating frequently. Bon appétit!

90. Cremini Mushroom Frittata with Cheese
(Ready in about 20 minutes | Servings 2)

This cheesy and veggie frittata is about to be your new favorite breakfast or brunch. Serve with Greek-style yogurt and ketchup.

Per serving: 282 Calories; 20.3g Fat; 7.7g Carbs; 17.6g Protein; 4.3g Sugars

Ingredients

1 tablespoon butter

1/2 cup Cremini mushrooms, sliced

1 bell pepper, seeded and chopped

1 serrano pepper, seeded and chopped

4 eggs

1 cup spinach, torn into pieces

Salt and ground black pepper, to taste

3 tablespoons milk

1/4 cup Colby cheese, shredded

Directions

- Grease the baking pan with melted butter. Add the mushrooms and peppers to the pan and cook at 350 degrees F for 6 minutes.
- In a mixing bowl, thoroughly combine the eggs with spinach, salt, black pepper, and milk. Add the mixture to the pan.
- Top with cheese and cook an additional 11 minutes. Cut into two slices and serve immediately.

91. Two-Cheese and Broccoli Quiche
(Ready in about 45 minutes | Servings 3)

This is not an average quiche recipe. Air fried and loaded with cheese, this quiche recipe is your ticket to Flavor Town!

Per serving: 276 Calories; 19g Fat; 8.9g Carbs; 18.3g Protein; 2.4g Sugars

Ingredients

1/2 head broccoli, broken into small
   florets
1 tomato, chopped
1/2 cup goat cheese, crumbled
1/2 cup sour cream

3 eggs, whisked
1/2 teaspoon smoked paprika
Salt and ground black pepper, to taste
1 cup Swiss cheese, shredded
1 tablespoon fresh chives, chopped

Directions

- Steam the broccoli for 18 minutes or until it is tender.
- Then, add the rinsed broccoli to a baking pan that is previously greased with a nonstick cooking spray.
- Add tomato and goat cheese. In a mixing bowl, thoroughly combine sour cream with eggs, paprika, salt, and black pepper.
- Next, pour the egg mixture into the pan. Scatter shredded Swiss cheese over the top.
- Cook in the preheated Air Fryer at 350 degrees F for 18 to 22 minutes. Serve garnished with fresh chives. Enjoy!

92. Quick and Easy Baked Eggs

(Ready in about 10 minutes | Servings 2)

This breakfast recipe is so easy to prepare that you will wonder how you have ever been without it and your Air Fryer. You can serve these eggs with Dijon mustard and spring onions as well.

Per serving: 225 Calories; 19.2g Fat; 4g Carbs; 16.3g Protein; 2.3g Sugars

Ingredients

2 eggs
1/4 teaspoon ground black pepper
1/4 teaspoon salt
1 teaspoon fresh parsley leaves,

chopped
2 slices of Cheddar cheese
1 tomato, sliced

Directions

- Preheat your Air Fryer to 320 degrees F. Spritz 2 ramekins with a nonstick cooking spray.
- Crack an egg into each ramekin; season with black pepper and salt. Bake for 5 to 6 minutes.
- Sprinkle with fresh parsley and serve with cheese and tomato. Bon appétit!

93. Fried Cheese and Kale Curds

(Ready in about 15 minutes | Servings 4)

You don't have to heat an oven to make the grainy and chewy cheese curds. If your mouths are already watering, give this recipe a try!

Per serving: 284 Calories; 18.7g Fat; 7.6g Carbs; 21.6g Protein; 1.9g Sugars

Ingredients

6 ounces mozzarella cheese

1 cup kale, blanched, drained and
   chopped

1/2 cup scallions, chopped

2 eggs

1/2 teaspoon garlic powder

1/2 teaspoon porcini powder

Kosher salt and ground black pepper,
   to taste

1/4 teaspoon cayenne pepper

3 teaspoons flaxseed meal

1/2 cup Parmesan cheese, grated

Directions

- In a mixing bowl, thoroughly combine all the ingredients, except Parmesan cheese. Mix until everything is well combined.
- Form into balls and roll into Parmesan cheese.
- Bake at 350 degrees F for 11 minutes. Serve warm or at room temperature. Enjoy!

94. Spicy Ham and Spinach Muffins
(Ready in about 15 minutes | Servings 3)

These low-carb muffins are absolutely perfect! You can pair these muffins with a dipping sauce like marinara and you'll have a delicious brunch or breakfast.

Per serving: 409 Calories; 27.9g Fat; 7.5g Carbs; 32.3g Protein; 3.6g Sugars

Ingredients

4 ounces smoked ham, chopped

1 bell pepper, chopped

1 habanero pepper, chopped

1 cup frozen spinach, chopped

4 ounces goat cheese, crumbled

4 eggs, whisked

Directions

- Divide smoked ham, peppers, and spinach between six silicone muffin molds. Add cheese and whisked eggs.
- Bake at 340 degrees F for 9 minutes. Allow them to cool for 5 minutes before removing from the molds.
- Serve with some extra sour cream or ketchup. Enjoy!

95. Vegetarian Cheese-Stuffed Peppers
(Ready in about 15 minutes | Servings 3)

This impressive vegetarian recipe is bursting with flavor. Ricotta cheese gives these peppers an unexpected creaminess. Enjoy!

Per serving: 223 Calories; 14.2g Fat; 9g Carbs; 14.6g Protein; 3.1g Sugars

Ingredients

3 bell peppers, deveined and halved

Salt, to taste

1 egg, whisked

6 ounces Ricotta cheese, at room temperature

2 ounces Parmesan cheese, grated

1/2 teaspoon red pepper flakes

Directions

- Sprinkle the peppers with salt.
- Mix the egg with Ricotta cheese; now, divide Ricotta mixture between peppers. Top with Parmesan cheese. Cook at 360 degrees F for 7 minutes.
- Serve at room temperature with a few sprinkles of red pepper flakes. Bon appétit!

96. Mushroom and Blue Cheese Tart
(Ready in about 30 minutes | Servings 4)

Tarts are so versatile! You can just add leftovers you have around your kitchen. In this recipe, we opted for mushrooms and leeks but you can come up with your unique combination!
Per serving: 314 Calories; 25.1g Fat; 4.9g Carbs; 17.4g Protein; 2.2g Sugars

Ingredients

4 eggs

1/2 cup heavy cream

1 cup blue cheese, crumbled

1 cup white mushrooms, chopped

1/4 teaspoon salt

1/4 teaspoon ground black pepper

A pinch of grated nutmeg

1/2 cup leeks, chopped

1 garlic clove, smashed

Directions

- In a mixing bowl, thoroughly combine the eggs and heavy cream.
- Add the remaining ingredients; mix until everything is well combined. Pour the mixture into a lightly greased baking pan.
- Cook in the preheated Air Fryer at 350 degrees for 28 minutes. Bon appétit!

VEGAN

97. Easy Spicy Broccoli
(Ready in about 15 minutes | Servings 4)

This easy and spicy broccoli is sure to please the whole family! Broccoli is a powerhouse of vitamins C, K, and E as well as dietary fiber and minerals.

Per serving: 96 Calories; 8.3g Fat; 4.2g Carbs; 3.8g Protein; 1.2g Sugars

Ingredients

1 pound broccoli, cut into florets

2 tablespoons olive oil

1 tablespoon Shoyu sauce

1 teaspoon hot sauce

Salt and ground black pepper, to taste

1 teaspoon paprika

Directions

- Preheat your Air Fryer to 395 degrees F. Brush broccoli florets with olive oil.
- Cook broccoli for 5 minutes.
- In a mixing bowl, whisk Shoyu sauce, hot sauce, salt, black pepper, and paprika.
- Toss this sauce with the prepared broccoli and pearl onions. Serve warm, garnished with nutritional yeast.

98. Dijon Mashed Rutabaga
(Ready in about 25 minutes | Servings 2)

This is a fun way to make dinner for two. Fancy and fluffy rutabaga mash with mustard and butter burst with flavors!

Per serving: 91 Calories; 4.2g Fat; 9.7g Carbs; 2.3g Protein; 6.6g Sugars

Ingredients

1/2 pound rutabaga, peeled and diced
1 teaspoon sea salt
1/2 teaspoon ground black pepper
1/4 teaspoon smoked paprika
Nonstick cooking spray

1/4 cup soy milk
2 tablespoons vegan margarine
1/2 teaspoon Dijon mustard
1 tablespoon fresh Italian parsley, chopped

Directions

- Season rutabaga with salt, black pepper, and smoked paprika. Spritz your rutabaga with a nonstick cooking spray.
- Cook the seasoned rutabaga for 18 minutes at 400 degrees F.
- Next, mash your rutabaga and add milk, margarine, and mustard. Mix until everything is well combined.
- Serve garnished with Italian parsley. Bon appétit!

99. Mushroom and Cauliflower Burgers
(Ready in about 35 minutes | Servings 4)

You can make a double batch and freeze your burgers for later. It's great to have healthy and delicious homemade burgers always on hand.

Per serving: 115 Calories; 7.6g Fat; 9g Carbs; 5.7g Protein; 4.2g Sugars

Ingredients

1 tablespoon canola oil

1/2 cup spring onions, finely chopped

1 garlic clove, smashed

1 bell pepper, chopped

1 teaspoon Habanero pepper, chopped

13 ounces mushrooms, chopped into
   small pieces

1/2 head cauliflower, grated

1/2 teaspoon ground cumin

6 tablespoons almond flour

Nonstick cooking spray

Directions

- Heat canola oil in a nonstick skillet that is preheated over a moderate flame.
- Sweat spring onions and garlic until tender and aromatic. Add the peppers; cook an additional 3 minutes or until tender.
- Now, add mushrooms and cauliflower; sauté an additional 4 minutes. Add cumin and almond flour.
- Shape the mixture into patties. Place them in your freezer for 20 minutes.
- Spritz your burgers with a nonstick cooking spray and bake them in the Air Fryer grill pan at 350 degrees F for 10 minutes. Serve with salsa and fresh lettuce. Enjoy!

100. Mushrooms with Sweet and Sour Sauce
(Ready in about 20 minutes | Servings 4)

Who doesn't love the comfort of biting into delicious stuffed mushrooms? Make a sweet and sour sauce for dunking and enjoy!

Per serving: 130 Calories; 7.3g Fat; 9.5g Carbs; 6.5g Protein; 4.2g Sugars

Ingredients

12 chestnut mushrooms, stalks removed

1 tablespoon olive oil

1/2 small-sized leek, chopped

2 garlic cloves, minced

1 bell pepper, chopped

1 teaspoon cayenne pepper

Sea salt and ground black pepper, to taste

2 tablespoons nutritional yeast flakes

1/2 cup water

1/2 cup tomato puree

1/4 cup Erythritol

1/4 cup seasoned vinegar

Directions

- Brush the mushrooms with olive oil. Stuff the mushrooms with leeks, garlic, and peppers.
- Now, sprinkle them with cayenne pepper, salt, and black pepper. Top with nutritional yeast flakes.
- Now, cook stuffed mushrooms in the preheated Air Fryer at 390 degrees F for 11 minutes.
- In a medium pan, simmer the remaining ingredients for the sauce until it has reduced and slightly thickened. Serve warm mushrooms with sweet and sour sauce on the side. Bon appétit!

101. Brussels Sprout Chips

(Ready in about 50 minutes | Servings 4)

Healthy vegan snacks are super easy to make in an Air Fryer. Most people can't resist Brussels sprout chips, it looks so light and crispy!

Per serving: 108 Calories; 7g Fat; 9.1g Carbs; 3.8g Protein; 2.4g Sugars

Ingredients

1 pound Brussels sprouts, thinly sliced

2 tablespoons olive oil, at room temperature

1/2 teaspoon ground cumin

1 teaspoon garlic powder

1/2 teaspoon salt

Directions

- Toss Brussels sprouts with olive oil, cumin, garlic powder, and salt.
- Cook at 400 degrees F for 9 minutes, shaking the basket halfway through cooking time.
- Let it cool before serving time and enjoy!

102. The Best Tofu Ever
(Ready in about 45 minutes | Servings 4)

Satisfy your sandwich craving in a flash! These amazing TLT (tofu, tomato and lettuce) sandwiches will win your heart.

Per serving: 173 Calories; 10.9g Fat; 8.1g Carbs; 14.1g Protein; 2.1g Sugars

Ingredients

12 ounces tofu, pressed and cubed

1 tablespoon Shoyu sauce

2 tablespoons tomato puree

1 teaspoon grated ginger, fresh or jarred

1 tablespoon olive oil

1 teaspoon dried thyme leaves, chopped

2 teaspoons arrowroot starch

4 fresh Boston lettuce leaves

2 medium-sized tomatoes, thinly sliced

Directions

- Place tofu in a mixing bowl. Add Shoyu sauce, tomato puree, ginger, olive oil, and thyme leaves; allow it to marinate for 20 minutes.
- Preheat the Air Fryer to 360 degrees F.
- Then coat the marinated tofu with the arrowroot starch. Cook for 23 minutes, shaking halfway through cooking time.
- Serve the prepared tofu with lettuce and tomato slices. Bon appétit!

103. Chips with Hot Peanut Butter Sauce

(Ready in about 20 minutes | Servings 2)

This is an Air Fryer classic! Olive oil can withstand higher heats, making your chips crisper and tastier.

Per serving: 330 Calories; 11.5g Fat; 63g Carbs; 10.5g Protein; 10.1g Sugars

Ingredients

3 cups purple kale

2 tablespoons olive oil

Salt, to taste

1/4 cup chunky peanut butter

1 teaspoon soy sauce

1 teaspoon hot sauce

Directions

- In a large bowl, toss the kale with olive oil and salt; transfer to your Air Fryer.
- Cook at 370 degrees F for 5 minutes, shaking halfway through cooking time.
- In the meantime, make the sauce by mixing peanut butter, soy sauce, and hot sauce.
- Serve warm chips with peanut butter sauce on the side. Bon appétit!

104. Spicy Roasted Green Beans

(Ready in about 25 minutes | Servings 4)

Green beans are among the healthiest foods in the world. They can improve your heart health, protect your immune system, regulate blood sugar, and so on.
Per serving: 68 Calories; 5.4g Fat; 4.6g Carbs; 0.7g Protein; 0.5g Sugars

Ingredients

10 ounces green beans, canned and drained
1 ½ tablespoons dark sesame oil
1/2 teaspoon cayenne pepper

1 teaspoon ground cumin
1 teaspoon chili powder
Salt and ground black pepper, to taste
1 ½ tablespoons lime juice

Directions

- Toss green beans with the remaining ingredients until evenly coated.
- Preheat your Air Fryer to 390 degrees F. Cook green beans for 16 minutes.
- Lower the temperature to 360 degrees F and cook an additional 4 minutes. Enjoy!

105. Pad Thai with Vegetable Sauce

(Ready in about 30 minutes | Servings 4)

Pad Thai is traditionally made with sugar. Add only 1/4 teaspoon of molasses for a keto-friendly version that is authentic and delicious too.

Per serving: 96 Calories; 7.2g Fat; 9.2g Carbs; 1.5g Protein; 4.1g Sugars

Ingredients

1/2 head Napa cabbage, shredded

2 tablespoons avocado oil

1/4 cup tamari sauce

1/4 teaspoon blackstrap molasses

1 teaspoon garlic puree

2 tablespoon fresh lime juice

1 bell pepper, chopped

Salt, to taste

1/4 teaspoon ground black pepper

1/4 teaspoon chili powder

1 teaspoon coriander paste

1/2 tablespoon Thai green curry paste

1 (7-ounce) package shirataki fettuccini noodles

2 spring onions, coarsely chopped

Directions

- Preheat your Air Fryer to 380 degrees F. Add shredded cabbage, avocado oil, tamari sauce, molasses, garlic puree and fresh lime juice to the Air Fryer.
- Cook for 10 minutes, shaking halfway through cooking time.
- Then, add bell pepper, salt, black pepper, chili powder, and coriander paste.
- Cook for 3 minutes more or until everything is cooked through. Stir in Thai green curry paste.
- Meanwhile, cook shirataki noodles until they are soft enough to eat, but still firm. Rinse noodles and transfer them to a serving bowl.
- Add cabbage mixture to the bowl; toss to combine and serve garnished with coarsely chopped spring onions.

106. Grilled Peppers with Vegan Aioli
(Ready in about 20 minutes | Servings 2)

Who wants to bother making a charcoal fire for one vegan meal? No worries, an Air Fryer will do the job. These grilled veggies will blow your mind!

Per serving: 252 Calories; 24.1g Fat; 9.3g Carbs; 2.2g Protein; 2.5g Sugars

Ingredients

Nonstick cooking spray

1 orange bell pepper, deveined and cut into four strips lengthwise

1 green bell pepper, deveined and cut into four strips lengthwise

1 sprig thyme, leaves picked

1 sprig rosemary, leaves picked

Flaky salt and ground black pepper, to taste

For Vegan Aioli:

1 small avocado, flesh scooped out

1 teaspoon Dijon mustard

1 tablespoon lemon juice

1/4 teaspoon salt

1/4 teaspoon black pepper

2 tablespoons olive oil

Directions

- Give your vegetables a generous spritz with a nonstick cooking spray.
- Sprinkle with thyme, rosemary, flaky salt and ground black pepper.
- Preheat your Air Fryer to 400 degrees F. Cook peppers in a grill pan for 12 minutes or until they are softened.
- To make vegan aioli, add the avocado, mustard, lemon, salt and black pepper to a food processor; blend until well combined.
- With the machine running, pour in olive oil. Mix until creamy and smooth.
- Serve grilled tomatoes and peppers with vegan aioli on the side. Enjoy!

107. Mexican Green Beans Ole

(Ready in about 20 minutes | Servings 4)

Green beans are an excellent source of antioxidants, vitamins, and minerals such as iron, potassium, manganese, and copper. They can improve digestion and heart, prevent colon cancer, and control diabetes.

Per serving: 135 Calories; 10.1g Fat; 9.7g Carbs; 4.2g Protein; 2g Sugars

Ingredients

1 teaspoon garlic powder

1 teaspoon chipotle powder

1/2 teaspoon cumin powder

Salt and red pepper, to taste

1/2 cup almond flour

1 (14.5-ounce) can green beans, drained

1/2 avocado, sliced

Directions

- Preheat your Air Fryer to 360 degrees F.
- In a mixing bowl, thoroughly combine garlic powder, chipotle powder, cumin, salt, red pepper, and almond flour.
- Dip green beans in the flour mixture.
- Cook for 8 minutes, shaking halfway through cooking time. Serve with avocado. Bon appétit!

108. Festive Zucchini Tortillas

(Ready in about 35 minutes | Servings 4)

Make zucchini tortillas for the next party and amaze your guests! These keto tortillas are versatile and convenient and they also add nutrition and unique flavor to your Air Fryer meals.

Per serving: 165 Calories; 13.9g Fat; 6.1g Carbs; 5.7g Protein; 0.7g Sugars

Ingredients

2 medium-sized zucchinis, grated

2 tablespoons flaxseeds, ground

1 tablespoon psyllium husk

2 tablespoons nutritional yeast

1/4 teaspoon cayenne pepper

Salt, to taste

1/2 cup almond flour

2 tablespoons vegan margarine

Directions

- Thoroughly combine all of the above ingredients in a mixing bowl.
- Mix until the batter forms a soft, pliable ball. Divide your batter into four balls.
- Cook at 390 degrees F for 20 minutes, working in batches. Serve with keto veggies if desired.

109. Asparagus with Green Dip

(Ready in about 25 minutes | Servings 4)

Asparagus is so widely available and easy to prepare. With a double-dip worthy sauce, it is perfect for a late night snack!

Per serving: 170 Calories; 14.9g Fat; 6.6g Carbs; 4.4g Protein; 3.7g Sugars

Ingredients

1 pound asparagus spears
1 ½ tablespoons sesame oil
1/2 teaspoon dried basil, crushed
1 teaspoon rosemary, chopped
1/2 teaspoon kosher salt

For the Dipping Sauce:
2 tablespoons watercress
2 tablespoons fresh flat-leaf parsley leaves
1 stalk green onion
1/2 cup non-dairy sour cream
1/4 cup vegan mayonnaise

Directions

- Begin by preheating your Air Fryer to 360 degrees F.
- Then, toss the asparagus with sesame oil, basil, rosemary, and salt.
- Cook for 6 minutes without shaking.
- While asparagus is cooking, prepare the sauce by mixing all of the sauce ingredients in a food processor. Pulse a couple of times or until everything is well incorporated.
- Serve the prepared veggie sticks with well-chilled dip. Bon appétit!

DESSERTS

110. Blood Orange and Ginger Cheesecake
(Ready in about 45 minutes | Servings 10)

Before beginning the recipe, check to make sure that the springform pan you plan to use fits into your Air Fryer. Enjoy!

Per serving: 201 Calories; 16.4g Fat; 8.4g Carbs; 6.3g Protein; 4.9 g Sugars

Ingredients

1 cup almond flour

1/2 stick butter, melted

7 ounces Neufchatel, at room temperature

1/4 cup sour cream

8 ounces erythritol, powdered

2 eggs

2 tablespoons orange juice

1 teaspoon orange peel, finely shredded

A pinch of salt

A pinch of freshly grated nutmeg

1 teaspoon ground star anise

1/2 teaspoon vanilla paste

2 large blood oranges

2 tablespoons crystallized ginger, finely chopped

Directions

- Start by preheating your Air Fryer to 350 degrees F for 5 minutes. Coat the inside of a springform pan with a baking paper.
- Then, in a mixing dish, thoroughly combine almond flour with butter. Press this crust into the bottom of the springform pan.
- In a mixing dish, thoroughly combine Neufchatel with sour cream and erythritol. Fold in the eggs, one at a time and continue to whisk this mixture.
- Add the orange juice and peel; add all seasonings. Spread this orange layer over the crust in the pan.
- Place the springform pan into your Air Fryer; cook for 13 minutes; then, cook for a further 13 minutes at 320 degrees F,
- Lastly, turn the temperature to 305 degrees F and cook an additional 17 minutes. Garnish with blood orange and crystallized ginger.
- Refrigerate overnight and serve well-chilled.

111. Traditional Tejeringos with Chocolate Sauce

(Ready in about 2 hours 25 minutes | Servings 8)

Easy to make and fun to eat, traditional Tejeringos is a decadent dessert you will love. You can make the dough the night before and save your time on an actual day.

Per serving: 175 Calories; 14.4g Fat; 9.4g Carbs; 3.3g Protein; 4.8g Sugars

Ingredients

1 ¼ cups almond flour
1/3 cup erythritol, powdered
1/2 teaspoon baking powder
1 teaspoon baking soda
1/2 teaspoon ground cardamom
1/4 teaspoon crystallized ginger
1/8 teaspoon grated nutmeg
A pinch of salt
1 egg white
1/3 cup ghee, melted
1/3 cup evaporated milk

For the Chocolate Sauce:
3 ounces cocoa powder, no sugar added
1 ounce coconut oil
1/2 cup heavy cream

Directions

- Thoroughly combine almond flour, erythritol, baking powder, baking soda, cardamom, ginger, nutmeg, and salt in a mixing bowl.
- Fold in the egg white, ghee, and milk, and whisk with a fork.
- Transfer the dough to your refrigerator for 2 hours. Cover the bottom of your Air Fryer with a sheet of baking paper.
- Knead the dough and transfer it to a pastry bag fitted with a large star tip. Pipe 4-inch long strips of dough into the cooking basket, without crowding; spritz with a nonstick cooking oil.
- Air fry at 365 degrees F for 7 minutes.
- To make the sauce, in a small-sized pan, warm the cocoa powder, coconut oil, and heavy cream. Serve the prepared Tejeringos with the chocolate sauce. Bon appétit!

112. Sunday Berry Cobbler

(Ready in about 20 minutes | Servings 2)

This sweet and aromatic berry cobbler is so easy to prepare in the Air Fryer. Moreover, it can be on your dessert table in just 20 minutes.

Per serving: 326 Calories; 32.5g Fat; 8.5g Carbs; 3.6g Protein; 2.6g Sugars

Ingredients

1 cups mixed berries

1/4 cup swerve

2 tablespoons butter, melted

1/4 teaspoon grated nutmeg

1/2 teaspoon ground cinnamon

1/3 teaspoon ground star anise

A pinch of coarse salt

1/3 cup almond flour

2 tablespoons coconut oil, room temperature

Directions

- Start by preheating your Air Fryer to 360 degrees F for 5 minutes.
- Toss apple slices with swerve, butter, nutmeg, cinnamon, star anise, and salt. Top with almond flour mixed with coconut oil.
- Cook for 14 minutes, shaking halfway through cooking time.
- Store in an airtight container and enjoy!

113. Winter Fruit and Nut Dessert

(Ready in about 45 minutes | Servings 5)

All you need is 45 minutes and a few simple ingredients for this nutty and fruity dessert. Easy and delicious with even five layers of flavor.

Per serving: 155 Calories; 12.6g Fat; 9.1g Carbs; 2.8g Protein; 5.2g Sugars

Ingredients

Nonstick cooking spray

2 cups blueberries

1/2 cup walnuts, ground

3/4 cup swerve

1/2 teaspoon ground cinnamon

3 teaspoons coconut oil, cold

1 cup heavy cream

Directions

- Begin by preheating your Air Fryer to 370 degrees F. Lightly spritz a baking pan with a nonstick cooking oil.
- Now, add a layer of blueberries. Sprinkle with walnuts, swerve, and cinnamon; repeat until you run out of ingredients.
- Crumb the coconut oil over the top and bake for 35 minutes or until syrupy. Allow it to sit at room temperature until it is firm enough to slice.
- Serve at room temperature, topped with heavy cream. Bon appétit!

115. Chocolate and Pecan Cupcakes

(Ready in about 25 minutes | Servings 12)

Here's a unique recipe for puffy, simple and elegant cupcakes. You can serve them on any occasion.

Per serving: 132 Calories; 10.8g Fat; 8.8g Carbs; 1.3g Protein; 4.1g Sugars

Ingredients

1/2 cup almond flour
1/2 teaspoon baking powder
2 tablespoons evaporated milk
1 stick butter, at room temperature
1/3 cup swerve

1/4 teaspoon cardamom
1/4 teaspoon grated nutmeg
2 tablespoons pecans, chopped
2 ounces low-carb chocolate chips

Directions

- Preheat your Air Fryer to 320 degrees F. Grease a muffin tin with a nonstick cooking spray.
- In a mixing bowl, sift the almond flour and baking powder.
- In another bowl, thoroughly combine the milk with butter, swerve, cardamom, and nutmeg. Fold in the chopped pecans and chocolate chips.
- Divide the mixture among muffin cups and transfer to your Air Fryer. Bake for 12 minutes.
- Turn off your Air Fryer and let the cupcakes sit for 8 minutes. Unmold your cupcakes and transfer them to a dessert platter. Bon appétit!

116. Grandma's Butter Rum Cookies
(Ready in about 25 minutes | Servings 10)

A butter rum flavoring gives a little kick to these amazingly delicious cookies. They will melt in your mouth.

Per serving: 211 Calories; 20.5g Fat; 4.2g Carbs; 3.3g Protein; 1.2g Sugars

Ingredients

1 cup almond flour
1 cup coconut flour
1 packet baking powder
1/2 teaspoon sea salt
1 stick butter, at room temperature

1 cup swerve
2 tablespoons buttermilk
2 tablespoons rum
1/2 teaspoon butter rum flavoring
2 ounces walnuts, finely chopped

Directions

- Begin by preheating the Air Fryer to 360 degrees F for 5 to 10 minutes.
- In a mixing dish, thoroughly combine the flour with baking powder and sea salt.
- Beat the butter and swerve with a hand mixer until pale and fluffy. Now, stir in the flour mixture.
- Add the remaining ingredients; mix to combine well. Divide the mixture into 14 small balls; flatten each ball with a fork and transfer them to a foil-lined baking pan.
- Put the baking pan into the Air Fryer and bake your cookies for 14 minutes. Work in a few batches, without crowding. Bon appétit!

117. Heavenly Chocolate Cake
(Ready in about 25 minutes | Servings 8)

Indulge yourself in this rich chocolate cake. It is perfect for an afternoon tea as well as an elegant dinner.

Per serving: 185 Calories; 15.9g Fat; 8.5g Carbs; 6.4g Protein; 1.9g Sugars

Ingredients

1/2 cup erythritol, powdered

1 stick butter, at room temperature

2 eggs, beaten

1 cup almond flour

1 teaspoon baking powder

2 teaspoons raw cocoa powder

1/2 teaspoon vanilla essence

1/8 teaspoon salt

1/8 teaspoon grated nutmeg

2 ounces unsweetened baker's chocolate

1 tablespoon heavy cream

1/4 cup fresh raspberries, to decorate

Directions

- Begin by preheating your Air Fryer to 320 degrees F. Spritz the inside of a baking pan with a nonstick cooking spray.
- Now, beat the erythritol and butter with an electric mixer until the mixture is creamy. Fold in the eggs and mix again.
- Then, add the flour, baking powder, cocoa powder, vanilla, salt, and nutmeg. Afterwards, stir in chocolate and heavy cream; mix to combine well.
- Scrape the batter into the prepared baking pan and level the surface using a spatula.
- Bake for 16 minutes or until a tester inserted in the center of your cake comes out dry. Decorate with fresh raspberries, cut into slices, and enjoy!

118. Best Ever Zucchini Cake
(Ready in about 40 minutes | Servings 8)

A perfect zucchini cake with the silkiest and smoothest frosting ever. Choosing a low carb lifestyle will help you reduce blood sugar, lose weight, and achieve an optimum health.
Per serving: 133 Calories; 12.6g Fat; 5.1g Carbs; 3.2g Protein; 1.5g Sugars

Ingredients

1 ¼ cups coconut flour
1 ½ teaspoons baking powder
1/2 teaspoon salt
4 tablespoons coconut oil
1/2 cup erythritol
2 eggs
1 zucchini
1/3 teaspoon cardamom
1/2 teaspoon ground star anise

For the Frosting:
2 ounces cream cheese
1/2 cup powdered erythritol
1 tablespoon butter, softened
2 tablespoons milk

Directions

- Start by preheating the Air Fryer to 325 degrees F for 5 minutes. Now, brush a baking pan with a butter-flavored nonstick cooking spray.
- In a mixing dish, thoroughly combine coconut flour with baking powder and salt.
- Beat coconut oil and erythritol until the mixture is smooth and uniform. Stir in the eggs and zucchini; mix again to combine well.
- Add the flour mixture, along with cardamom and anise. Mix again.
- Spoon the batter into the baking pan. Transfer to the preheated Air Fryer and bake for 35 minutes. Transfer to a wire rack to cool completely.
- Meanwhile, make the frosting by mixing the remaining ingredients. Frost your cake and enjoy!

119. Sponge Cake with Cherry Curd

(Ready in about 1 hour | Servings 10)

This recipe is so versatile. When it comes to the filling for this sponge cake, opt for your favorite filling like whipped cream, jam and so on.

Per serving: 254 Calories; 24.7g Fat; 4.4g Carbs; 5.2g Protein; 2.3g Sugars

Ingredients

Nonstick cooking spray
1 ½ sticks butter
1 1/3 cup erythritol
2 eggs
1 cup almond flour
1/2 teaspoon baking powder
1/2 teaspoon ground star anise
1 teaspoon vanilla extract

For the Filling:
2 eggs, whisked
1 tablespoon fresh lemon juice
1/4 teaspoon crystallized ginger
1 cup erythritol
8 ounces cherries, pitted
1 ½ ounces butter, unsalted

Directions

- Begin by preheating your Air Fryer to 360 degrees F. Then spritz two baking pans with a nonstick cooking spray.
- Beat 1 ½ sticks of butter and 1 1/3 cup of erythritol until the mixture is creamy and fluffy. Crack the eggs in and continue to mix until pale and smooth.
- Now, sift in the flour; add the baking powder, star anise, and vanilla extract.
- Scrape the batter into the prepared baking pan and bake for 15 minutes. Turn the temperature to 340 degrees F and bake for a further 10 minutes or until a skewer inserted into the middle of your cake comes out dry.
- Allow it to cool on a wire rack. Repeat with another cake.
- Place a glass bowl over a pot of boiling water. Add the whisked eggs, lemon juice, ginger, and 1 cup erythritol; mix to combine.
- Now, add cherries and 1 ½ ounces of unsalted butter to the bowl, stirring constantly about 18 minutes. The curd will harden as it cools.
- Place the first cake on a serving platter. Spread the filling over the cake and then, top with other cake. Bon appétit!

120. Christmas Mint Chocolate Cake
(Ready in about 20 minutes | Servings 10)

Looking for a perfect Christmas cake? Look no further, this cake is sure to please. Ho-ho-ho!
Per serving: 214 Calories; 17.1g Fat; 4.5g Carbs; 3.6g Protein; 2.3g Sugars

Ingredients

1 cup almond flour
1/2 cup coconut flour
1 ½ teaspoons baking powder
1/2 teaspoon kosher salt
1 ½ cups powdered erythritol
2 tablespoons raw cocoa powder

1 stick butter
2 eggs
3 tablespoons double cream
1/2 teaspoon mint extract
1 ounce baking chocolate, chopped into chunks

Directions

- Begin by preheating your Air Fryer to 360 degrees F. Lightly grease a baking pan.
- In a mixing bowl, thoroughly combine the flour, baking powder, and salt. Add powdered erythritol and cocoa; mix to combine.
- Cut in the butter and stir again.
- In another bowl, mix the eggs with double cream; add this mixture to the bowl with the flour mixture.
- Lastly, add mint extract and chocolate; mix to combine well. Scrape the batter into the prepared baking pan.
- Bake for 10 minutes or until a skewer inserted into the middle of your cake comes out dry. Bon appétit!

121. Old-Fashioned Fruit Tart
(Ready in about 30 minutes | Servings 8)

With its flaky crust, tart-sweet autumn fruits, and amazing ginger aroma, a slice of fruit tart is the perfect end to any meal. Enjoy!

Per serving: 191 Calories; 17.2g Fat; 8.1g Carbs; 4.4g Protein; 3.5g Sugars

Ingredients

1 cup almond flour
1/3 cup vegetable shortening
1/4 cup powdered erythritol
4 tablespoons evaporated milk
1 cup cherries

1/3 cup almonds, chopped
1 teaspoon apple pie spice mix
1/4 teaspoon crystallized ginger
A pinch of salt

Directions

- Start by preheating your Air Fryer to 360 degrees F.
- Combine the flour and vegetable shortening until the mixture is evenly crumbly. Now, stir in the powdered erythritol. Next, pour in the milk and mix until the dough is moist enough to hold together when you squeeze it.
- Divide the dough into two balls. Now, roll out the dough ball to make a "pastry shell" and fill your pan. Now, trim the edges so they overlap the rim of the pan by 1-inch all the way around.
- Add the cherries and almonds. Sprinkle them with apple pie spice mix, crystallized ginger, and salt.
- Roll out other ball and top your pie. Dot the top with the diced butter.
- Bake for 20 minutes or until thoroughly cooked. Remove your tart to a wire rack to cool completely. Bon appétit!

122. The Ultimate Chocolate and Almond Muffins
(Ready in about 30 minutes | Servings 6)

This is an easy recipe for everyday dessert. However, for special occasions, you can take the recipe to the next level and decorate your muffins with marshmallow frosting or buttercream.

Per serving: 330 Calories; 21.5g Fat; 9.2g Carbs; 7.8g Protein; 2g Sugars

Ingredients

1/2 stick unsalted butter

2 ounces baker's chocolate, unsweetened

2 tablespoons heavy cream

1/2 cup powdered erythritol

1/2 teaspoon vanilla extract

1/2 teaspoon ground cinnamon

A pinch of freshly grated nutmeg

A pinch of pinch salt

2 eggs

1 cup almond flour

Directions

- Start by preheating your Air Fryer to 340 degrees F. Line a muffin tin with paper liners.
- In a mixing bowl, thoroughly combine all of the above ingredients. Scrape the batter into the cups.
- Bake for 11 minutes or until a skewer inserted into the middle of your muffin comes out dry. Transfer to a wire rack to cool for 15 to 20 minutes before unmolding.
- Arrange on a serving plate. Bon appétit!

OTHER AIR FRYER FAVORITES

123. Mixed Berry Crumble

(Ready in about 30 minutes | Servings 6)

You'll never eat a fruit crumble the same way again after tasting this recipe. You can use seasonal berries of choice.

Per serving: 154 Calories; 13.2g Fat; 8.2g Carbs; 2.7g Protein; 2.9g Sugars

Ingredients

1/2 cup almond flour
1/3 cup coconut flour
3/4 cup monkfruit sweetener
1 ½ teaspoons cream of tartar

1/2 stick butter
2 chayote, chopped
1 cup berries

Directions

- Preheat your Air Fryer to 340 degrees F.
- Add flour, sweetener, cream of tartar, and butter to your food processor; mix until everything is well combined.
- Arrange chayote and berries in the bottom of a baking dish. Spread the butter/flour topping over the fruits.
- Bake for 20 minutes or until lightly browned. Serve at room temperature with a dollop of whipped cream. Bon appétit!

124. Colby Cheese and Prosciutto Muffins
(Ready in about 25 minutes | Servings 2)

The only thing better than a regular muffin is an air-fried muffin! Eat your ultimate comfort food in a completely new way.

Per serving: 448 Calories; 28.2g Fat; 7.5g Carbs; 40.2g Protein; 4.4g Sugars

Ingredients

4 eggs

1/2 cup buttermilk

4 ounces Coby cheese, shredded

4 ounces prosciutto, chopped

Directions

- Start by preheating your Air Fryer to 340 degrees F.
- Whisk the eggs and buttermilk in a bowl. Add Colby cheese and prosciutto. Divide the mixture among muffin cups.
- Cook for 15 minutes, turning halfway through. Eat warm.

125. Pizza with Peppers and Cheese
(Ready in about 25 minutes | Servings 2)

Follow these easy directions for creating a chewy, cheesy and veggie pizza at home. We opted for this version but you can come up with your favorite combo!

Per serving: 357 Calories; 27.3g Fat; 6.9g Carbs; 23g Protein; 3.7g Sugars

Ingredients

2 large eggs

2 tablespoons Parmesan cheese, grated

1 tablespoon psyllium husk powder

1 teaspoon dried oregano

A pinch of salt

1 tablespoon olive oil

1 bell pepper, deveined and thinly sliced

4 olives, pitted and sliced

1 teaspoon Italian seasoning

1/4 teaspoon salt

1/2 cup prosciutto, chopped

1/2 cup cheddar cheese, grated

1/2 cup Romano cheese, grated

Directions

- In a mixing bowl, thoroughly combine the eggs, Parmesan, psyllium husk, oregano, salt, and olive oil.
- To make pizza crust, heat a pan over medium-high heat. Spoon this mixture into the pan and spread out into a circle shape. Once the edges have started to set, flip it and bake on the other side for 1 minute more.
- Preheat your Air Fryer to 340 degrees F. Place a sheet of foil on the bottom of the cooking basket. Spritz with a nonstick cooking spray.
- Place the pizza on the bottom of the cooking basket. Add the remaining ingredients as a topping and bake for 10 minutes, until cheese is lightly browned. Bon appétit!

126. Easy Cheesy Muffins

(Ready in about 10 minutes | Servings 2)

Here is a super-fast breakfast recipe to jump-start your day. Add some other types of cheese if you'd like and discover new flavorful combinations.

Per serving: 316 Calories; 23.6g Fat; 2.2g Carbs; 20.1g Protein; 0.7g Sugars

Ingredients

4 eggs, beaten

3 ounces Monetary-Jack cheese, shredded

1/2 tablespoon butter, melted

1 teaspoon shallot powder

1 teaspoon garlic powder

1 teaspoon dried basil

Directions

- Preheat your Air Fryer to 340 degrees F.
- Mix all of the above ingredients until everything is well combined. Now, spoon the mixture into silicone muffin cups.
- Cook for 6 minutes or until they are slightly browned and set. These muffins can be stored in the refrigerator for at least a week. Bon appétit!

127. Mushroom and Goat Cheese Omelet
(Ready in about 20 minutes | Servings 2)

A cheese and vegetable omelet is always a great idea. It sounds like a romantic and delicious breakfast for two!
Per serving: 360 Calories; 26.8g Fat; 8.4g Carbs; 22.1g Protein; 4.3g Sugars

Ingredients

4 eggs

1 tablespoon butter, softened

4 tablespoons goat cheese, crumbled

Sea salt and ground black pepper, to
   your liking

1 teaspoon olive oil

1 cup white mushrooms, thinly sliced

1 teaspoon fresh garlic, minced

2 tablespoons red onion, chopped

1/4 teaspoon red pepper flakes

Directions

- Preheat your Air Fryer to 360 degrees F.
- Beat the eggs in a mixing dish; add the butter and cheese; mix again to combine. Season with salt and pepper and set the mixture aside.
- Next, heat the olive oil in a frying pan over a moderate flame. Cook the mushrooms together with garlic and red onions until the vegetables have softened, about 4 minutes.
- Add the sautéed vegetables to the egg mixture; mix again to combine well. Cook for 14 minutes in your Air Fryer.
- Afterwards, divide your omelet between two serving plates. Sprinkle with add red pepper flakes and serve immediately.

128. Sausages with Horseradish Sauce
(Ready in about 25 minutes | Servings 4)

Everyone likes budget-friendly meals, right? Sausages are one of the best options when you want to please your family and stay on budget.

Per serving: 378 Calories; 33g Fat; 6.2g Carbs; 13.2g Protein; 1.1g Sugars

Ingredients

4 Aberdeen sausages, skinless
1/2 cup yellow onion, chopped

For the Horseradish Sauce:
1/2 cup sour cream
2 tablespoons fresh horseradish, grated
1/2 tablespoon Dijon mustard
Salt and pepper, to taste

Directions

- Begin by preheating your Air Fryer to 380 degrees F.
- Add sausages to a grill pan and cook them for 20 minutes, turning once or twice.
- In the meantime, make the sauce by whisking all of the sauce ingredients.
- Divide the grilled sausages between four plates. Serve with fresh chopped onion and horseradish sauce. Bon appétit!

129. Tex-Mex Beef Burritos

(Ready in about 15 minutes | Servings 2)

Here's the recipe for a Mexican classic – a tortilla stuffed with a simple beef filling. Serve with a dollop of sour cream.

Per serving: 456 Calories; 34.1g Fat; 9g Carbs; 27.8g Protein; 4.9g Sugars

Ingredients

1 teaspoon olive oil
1/2 onion, finely chopped
2 garlic cloves
4 ounces ground beef
1 tablespoon tomato puree
Salt and pepper, to taste

4 eggs
1/3 cup coconut flour
1/2 teaspoon baking powder
2 tablespoons heavy cream
2 tablespoons butter, melted

Directions

- Heat the oil in a nonstick pan over a medium-high heat. Now, sauté the onion and garlic until the onion is lightly browned.
- Add ground beef and cook until it is no longer pink, about 5 minutes. Then, stir in tomato puree and cook an additional minute or until everything is cooked through. Season with salt and pepper to taste.
- To make your tortillas, simply mix the eggs with flour, baking powder, and heavy cream.
- Grease the cooking basket with melted butter.
- Bake tortillas at 390 degrees F for 15 minutes, working in batches. Stuff each tortilla with reserved beef mixture and enjoy!

130. Ranch and Bacon Peppers
(Ready in about 20 minutes | Servings 5)

Here's an easy and creative way to make a satisfying snack for your guests. Fresh coriander provides a depth of herbal flavor, while powdered ranch seasoning completes the meal with its extraordinary, rich notes.

Per serving: 430 Calories; 44.4g Fat; 5.8g Carbs; 2.1g Protein; 3.1g Sugars

Ingredients

1/3 cup cream cheese, at room temperature

1 tablespoon powdered ranch seasoning

3 tablespoons fresh coriander, finely chopped

5 mini peppers, deveined

10 bacon strips

Directions

- Preheat your Air Fryer to 380 degrees F.
- Mix cream cheese with powdered ranch seasoning and coriander. Cut the peppers into halves; fill them with the cheese mixture.
- Wrap each half of pepper with a bacon strip and secure with a toothpick. Cook in the preheated Air Fryer for 12 minutes. Bon appétit!

131. French Mini Egg Frittatas
(Ready in about 15 minutes | Servings 2)

Start the day right with this old-fashioned favorite! Serve with yogurt, sour cream or bacon.
Per serving: 479 Calories; 40g Fat; 1.9g Carbs; 27.8g Protein; 0.7g Sugars

Ingredients

2 tablespoons butter, softened

4 eggs

1/8 teaspoon freshly grated nutmeg

1/4 teaspoon ground black pepper

1 cup Comté cheese, crumbled

1 cup spinach, chopped

Directions

- Preheat your Air Fryer to 360 degrees F.
- Mix the butter, eggs, nutmeg, black pepper, cheese and spinach in a mixing dish. Now, spoon the mixture into silicone muffin cups.
- Bake at 340 degrees F for 9 minutes. Allow them to cool for 5 minutes before removing from the silicone muffin cups. Enjoy!

132. English Muffin Toasts with Eggs

(Ready in about 13 minutes | Servings 2)

The crunchy texture of these sinfully delicious muffin toasts makes them perfect for dipping into an air-fried egg yolk.

Per serving: 464 Calories; 42.6g Fat; 7.3g Carbs; 15.3g Protein; 2.6g Sugars

Ingredients

6 tablespoons almond flour

1 tablespoon coconut flour

1 teaspoon baking powder

2 tablespoons ghee, at room temperature

4 eggs, whisked

1/2 teaspoon salt

2 tablespoons butter

1/4 cup hot spicy ketchup

Directions

- Thoroughly combine almond flour and coconut flour; add baking powder, ghee, 2 eggs, and salt.
- Divide this batter into 2 balls and flatten them slightly. Microwave for about 90 seconds or until firm.
- Butter two ramekins. Crack the remaining 2 eggs into ramekins. Cook for 5 minutes at 390 degrees F. Season the eggs to taste.
- Serve warm English muffins them with eggs and hot spicy ketchup. Bon appétit!

133. Easy Avocado Chips
(Ready in about 15 minutes | Servings 4)

Make sure to choose underripe avocados for this addictive and healthy snack. Feel free to double the recipe!

Per serving: 173 Calories; 13.2g Fat; 8.1g Carbs; 7.1g Protein; 1.3g Sugars

Ingredients

1/3 teaspoon garlic powder

1/3 teaspoon salt

1/4 teaspoon black pepper

1 large-sized avocado, peeled, pitted
   and sliced

3/4 cup Parmesan cheese, grated

1/3 cup plain milk

1/2 teaspoon turmeric powder

Directions

- Season avocado slices with garlic powder, salt, and black pepper.
- Add Parmesan cheese in a shallow dish. Place the milk and turmeric powder in another dish.
- Dip each avocado slice in the milk mixture. Roll each slice into grated Parmesan cheese, pressing down lightly until your crumbs stick well.
- Bake the breaded avocado slices in a single layer for 12 minutes at 390 degrees F. Work in batches, turning halfway through cooking time to ensure they are cooking evenly.
- Serve at room temperature. Bon appétit!

134. Shrimp with Avocado Salsa

(Ready in about 20 minutes | Servings 2)

The title says it all. Warm shrimp and sautéed vegetables accompanied by zingy avocado salsa and a dollop of sour cream!

Per serving: 274 Calories; 15.7g Fat; 9.8g Carbs; 23.4g Protein; 4.1g Sugars

Ingredients

1 tablespoon olive oil

2 garlic cloves, smashed

1 bell pepper, deveined and thinly sliced

1 Serrano pepper, deveined and finely chopped

10 medium shrimp, peeled and deveined

2 dollops of sour cream

For the Avocado Salsa:

1 tomato, chopped

1/2 avocado, peeled, seeded and cut into chunks

1 chili pepper, seeded and chopped

1/4 teaspoon salt

1/4 teaspoon ground black pepper

1/2 tablespoon fresh lime juice

2 tablespoons fresh cilantro leaves, coarsely chopped

Directions

- Heat the oil in a sauté pan that is preheated over a moderate heat. Now, sauté the garlic and peppers until they're softened.
- Now, preheat your Air Fryer to 390 degrees F; cook your shrimp for 5 minutes or until thoroughly cooked. Add the shrimp to the sautéed vegetable.
- Meanwhile, prepare the salsa by mixing all of the salsa ingredients. Serve shrimp and veggies with a dollop of sour cream and the fresh salsa. Bon appétit!

135. Traditional Sicilian Arancini
(Ready in about 40 minutes | Servings 6)

Arancini with two types of cheese, seasoning, and pine nuts are a gourmet's dream. This is a great way to turn leftover cauli rice into elegant golden balls as well.

Per serving: 166 Calories; 11.7g Fat; 3.1g Carbs; 12.1g Protein; 1.1g Sugars

Ingredients

- 1 ½ cups cauliflower
- 3 eggs, beaten
- 3 ounces Romano cheese, grated
- 2 ounces Fontina cheese, shredded
- 1/4 teaspoon cayenne pepper
- 1/2 teaspoon freshly ground black pepper
- 1/2 teaspoon salt
- 1 teaspoon onion powder
- 1/2 teaspoon garlic powder
- 2 tablespoons pine nuts, toasted and ground
- 2 packets sage and onion stuffing mix

Directions

- Pulse the cauliflower in a food processor; process until broken down into rice-size pieces.
- Add the eggs, Romano cheese, Fontina cheese, cayenne pepper, ground black pepper, salt, onion powder, garlic powder, and pine nuts. Cover and chill for 1 hour.
- Now, stir in the egg mixture; stir until everything is well incorporated. Spread on a parchment-lined cookie sheet to cool completely.
- Shape the mixture into bite-sized balls.
- Add the sage and onion stuffing mix to a shallow dish. Roll the balls into the sage and onion stuffing mix and transfer them to a cooking basket; spritz them with a nonstick cooking spray.
- Cook at 350 degrees F for 15 minutes or until crisp and golden. Bon appétit!

45348467R00087

Made in the USA
Columbia, SC
20 December 2018